ADVANCED PRAISE FOR MADRE

"The elements of this book highlight the admirable work of a woman who embraced the crucifix... and worked to show the face of God in the midst of her every work.... I hope that the life and works of this servant of the Lord serve as an inspiration for every Christian and person of good will who feels called to do good for a more just society."

—*Cardinal Óscar Andrés Rodriguez Maradiaga, S.D.B., Archbishop of Tegucigalpa*

☙❧

"This is a powerful story of one woman's exploration of the deepest desires in her heart and their connection to the needs and challenges of the world. As Kathy Martin O'Neil guides us through the extraordinary journey of Sister María Rosa, she also enlightens the way God meets us in the ordinary moments of our own journeys. In the process, she helps us trust the unique calling of each and every person and the mission to be witness to light and hope amidst the darkness of the world."

—*Father Daniel Groody, C.S.C., Vice President and Associate Provost at the University of Notre Dame, editor of* A Promised Land, A Perilous Journey: Theological Perspectives on Migration *and author of* Globalization, Spirituality & Justice: Navigating a Path to Peace

۞

"Even if I had never known Sister María Rosa, this book conveys her so well as creative, prayerful, funny, faith-filled, genuinely caring, determined (occasionally called stubborn), and hospitable to us *Norteamericanos*, on whom she made a huge impact."

—*Father Jeffrey Godecker, founder of the Honduras outreach mission at Immaculate Heart of Mary parish in Indianapolis*

۞

"Sister María Rosa Leggol was God's rebel, with an ability to turn the impossible into reality. She cared for more children than her Board of Directors told her she could cope with, she saved children of mothers suffering deep psychiatric problems, she nursed malnourished and unloved children back to health. No one could say 'no' to this extraordinary Honduran nun. Kathy Martin O'Neil has talked to many volunteers who came down to Honduras on a week's volunteer mission and remained close to Sister María Rosa for decades thereafter, becoming advisors, 'spiritual boyfriends,' and godparents of countless Honduran children. I am one of them. On a cold January morning in 1982, I went to Sister

María Rosa for advice. My husband and I had been married for 7 years and had failed to produce a child. Filled with understanding, she listened and made a call to the clinic. A few hours later I took home an 8-month-old bundle, Marina. The two U.S. congressmen staying at our home ran out to buy a cloth donkey and elephant, representing their respective political parties. Over the next 11 years, Sister María Rosa transferred her care of several children to us. We remain proud to support God's rebel, who 'rode her Holy Spirit over a deep, dark lake of poverty and need... committed to the lifelong battle to bring hope and dignity to the poor.'" —*Diana Negroponte*

❧

"In *Madre*, Sister María Rosa's life story offers us a roadmap for following God's will in our lives. Her mission to save at-risk children motivates us in the same way as Mother Teresa, who said, 'Holiness consists in accepting, with a smile, what Jesus sends us.' This book will bring a smile to your face many times as it helps you accept and follow God's will for your life!"

—*Doctor Chuck Dietzen, founder of Timmy Global Health and author of* Pint-Sized Prophets: Inspirational Moments That Taught Me We Are All Born To Be Healers

MADRE

The Nun Who Was Mother to the Orphans of Honduras

KATHY MARTIN O'NEIL

Foreword by
CARDINAL ÓSCAR ANDRÉS RODRÍGUEZ
MARADIAGA

CORNELIA
AVENUE PRESS

Paperback ISBN: 978-1-7377263-0-2
Ebook ISBN: 978-1-7377263-1-9
Library of Congress Control Number: 2021915974
First print edition, 2022
First ebook edition, 2022

Cover design: Peter Selgin
Cover photograph: David Mangurian
Editor: Greg Cliburn

Excerpt of *Intelligence Reframed*, by Howard Gardner (New York: Basic
Books, 1999) reprinted by permission of the author.

CORNELIA
AVENUE PRESS

6101 North Keystone Ave. Suite 100 #1221,
Indianapolis, IN 46220
www.corneliaavenuepress.com

To my family in the United States by blood, marriage, and adoption, and in Honduras by the bonds of amistad, cariño y amor

CONTENTS

FOREWORD

"You are the light of the world. A city built on the top of a mountain cannot be hidden." —*Matthew 5:14*

Sister María Rosa Leggol (1926-2020) has been the most recognized religious person in Honduras. This is due to all the projects she has carried out in favor of orphaned and abandoned children. She said that she asked the Lord always for light, strength, power and intelligence. She did not ask to be famous or recognized, but to be able to visualize how each person could be changed, improved and illuminated through the light, joy, mercy and love of the Lord.

During 2020, the year in which the COVID-19 pandemic hit Honduras, Sister María Rosa did everything in her power to help the poorest people in the country with food and medicine. She did this even as she herself fought this terrible disease, which caused absolute weakness in her health until October 16 of the same year, when the Lord called her to His presence, plunging the hearts of the Honduran people into mourning.

The news of her death was quickly spread by all religious and civil media, demonstrating the importance of this woman in the nation. The mission that Sister María Rosa carried out in the Honduran population is admirable, so much so that, at the time of her departure, all her spiritual children and acquaintances began to highlight all the ways in which they were welcomed by their "Mother," as they affectionately call her.

It should also be noted that thousands of Hondurans tirelessly raised prayers for the soul of Sister María Rosa, even without having known her personally. However, they did know about many of her projects that became a mountain of light for Honduras.

More than a year after her departure, she continues to be fondly remembered, not only for the projects she carried out —fruit of the works of her hands—but above all because of the quality of her testimony of life for each one of us.

Sister María Rosa was a woman who was aware of her call from an early age. She was six years old when her mother died, and that same year she met the nuns who would mark her for her entire life. From this we realize that this woman from a very young age not only knew the taste of victory, but also knew the bitterness of the dark night, and thus she was building each project and mission that the Lord was entrusting to her between tears and laughter.

In truth, the vocation of this woman is firmly based on God, because she said, "You cannot go to a store to buy parts for a vocation. The Lord gives the vocation to you." She also advised that when there was weakness in her vocation, it was necessary to ask the Lord for that calling again and He would strengthen those who cried out to Him.

Sister María Rosa always focused on the most deprived,

orphaned children, unemployed parents, and homeless families. She was a woman who had a full vision of reality concentrated on helping society in an integral way, creating jobs, building houses, schools and health centers. But above all she worked to show the face of God in the midst of her every work.

It is said that Sister María Rosa helped more than 80,000 children and adolescents throughout her life, but really only God knows the full scope that this admirable woman has had and will have with each and every one of the projects that she has left as a legacy for our country.

The elements of this book have been designed to highlight the admirable work of a woman who embraced the crucifix and gave herself totally to the Lord with the vows of poverty, chastity and obedience. She came to the end of her life full of love and with a huge harvest of so much affection that she poured out on behalf of others. I hope that the life and works of this servant of the Lord serve as an inspiration for every Christian and person of good will who feels called to do good for a more just society.

—*Cardinal Óscar Andrés Rodríguez Maradiaga, S.D.B.,*
Archbishop of Tegucigalpa

PROLOGUE
MISSION TRIP EPIPHANIES

--"The dignity of life is to work, not to beg."--
—Sister María Rosa Leggol

Sister María Rosa Leggol was a dauntless Honduran woman on a crusade to rescue and raise abandoned, at-risk children in her country. Her story is an enthralling tale of victory against enormous odds, of light triumphing over darkness, and of love winning out over violence, machismo, and poverty. I could sense this even in the abridged version of her adventures I heard the first time I met her, in 2008, on my first mission trip to Honduras. So many years later, I remember feeling awestruck by (and perhaps initially a little skeptical of) her fearlessness and her invincible faith—a faith with the reputation of sparking divine intervention sometimes when she crucially needed it.

Over half a century of building homes, schools, farms, and clinics and launching other projects to help the poor, she raised the hopes and prospects of tens of thousands of vulnerable children and single mothers. To fully appreciate her unlikely success at transforming the lives of both Hondurans and the North American mission travelers who flock down to join her work, it's helpful to know the setting and to sense what it's like to meet Sister María Rosa on her home turf.

I didn't know what to expect of that first mission trip with my Catholic parish from Indianapolis, Indiana, but I was game for anything: medical and food brigades, construction and painting, dance parties and movie nights with the children of Sociedad Amigos de los Niños (SAN, the Society of the Friends of Children), Sister María Rosa's child rescue organization. At home I got shots and pills to ward off malaria, typhoid, and other diseases long eradicated here at home. I packed two large 50-pound suitcases full of children's vitamins, socks and underwear, sheets and towels, backpacks, deflated soccer balls, flip-flops, kids' clothing, toys and toothbrushes. I made a few meals for the freezer at home, arranged rides for my kids' extracurriculars, slept a few quick hours, and convened with my group at the Indianapolis airport at 4:30 a.m.

We flew into Tegucigalpa, a Third World capital city

sprawled slapdash across a wide bowl rimmed with jumbled green mountains. From a window seat I experienced the infamous landing at Toncontin Airport, when the plane banks sideways in a crazy, sharp U-turn toward a tiny ribbon of runway. My stomach banked sharply too, until we touched down safely and broke out in traditional applause for the pilot. From then on, my stomach fluttered instead with anticipation: I could not wait to meet Sister María Rosa, famous both in Honduras and in my church at home as a mother to orphaned and abandoned children.

We filed off the plane into blinding sunshine on the hot tarmac and wove through the Customs line. We wandered around the chaos of baggage claim until our local hostess ushered our group and our dozens of large suitcases out of the airport to a bus we'd rented for the week. I threaded my way through pockets of children and waiting families in the airport lobby. A very young boy ran up calling *"Foto! Foto,"* asking me to pay to snap his picture, and two elderly women begged with open hands and entreaties I could not understand with my lousy Spanish. We drove away from the airport in a cacophony of horns, squeezing our eyes shut at near-crashes in frenetic traffic with no discernible lanes. There were hints of a demonstration nearby—shouts of a crowd, the stench of burning tires—but our driver steered us clear of trouble or danger, a hallmark of the care and extreme caution with which Sister María Rosa's people shepherd the North American mission groups.

As we arrived at SAN headquarters, my questions about Sister María Rosa were silly, but still nagging: *Did she really raise tens of thousands of kids? Does she actually make time to meet and talk with the mission groups? What it's like to hobnob with someone so holy?* The trip veterans recounted a list of SAN's projects, the geographic layout of the children's village, the lore and traditions of the annual Immaculate Heart of Mary parish trip, the names of their favorite children there. All my queries about Sister María Rosa, though, were answered with this: "She will be declared a saint someday!"

(This theme always irked Sister María Rosa, by the way. In 2007, John L. Allen Jr. wrote in a *National Catholic Reporter* article that Sister María Rosa is called "the Mother Teresa of Honduras." Whether or not he was first to say it, the name stuck and became popular throughout Honduras and with mission groups trying to succinctly convey her celebrity. In frustration Sister María Rosa countered to me once, "I am not the saint you think; I am a rebellious old lady!" She firmly rejected comparison with Saint Teresa of Calcutta. "Mother Teresa was such a holy person, helping people learn how to die. I am supposed to be helping kids learn how to live," she said. "We are doing such different things! Lots of times I pray, 'Mother Teresa, I am sorry that the people are saying I am like you!'")

I expected to feel dazed in her hallowed presence, to see a lofty aura around her with her wise words shimmering in the air. Instead, my snapshot impression of Sister María Rosa was accompanied by a song title that popped into my head: "Bright Giant Love Ball," from Carey Landry's 1973 children's music album *Hi God*. She had just entered the dining room of her Tegucigalpa compound to say hello to our mission group as we devoured a hot lunch of beans, rice, (mystery) meat, and handmade tortillas. She held her arms out wide in welcome beneath a huge open-mouthed smile. She was short, stout, and bouncy on her feet, a round ball of light, humor, and warmth that made me want to giggle. (I actually did giggle when she announced to us that the O.S.F.

acronym after her name did not signify "Order of Saint Francis," but in her case meant "Oh so fat.") She had a bright and shining presence, but it wasn't sacrosanct or superior. Rather, that light attracted me toward her happy mood, her fuzzy brown cheek to kiss. I would know her formidable strength and orneriness soon enough, but on my first meeting she exuded warm humanity and gentle humility.

Her habit that day was white (though she alternately wore brown, tan, or blue): a loose cotton dress adorned with a single large pin of Our Lady of Fatima that said "Salvadme Reina Fatima 1917." On her right hand she wore a wedding ring from her Franciscan community, which was stolen several years later by robbers who climbed in the window of her bedroom. She wore slippers on red, swollen feet (a result of lymphedema) and a black veil from which wispy white hairs escaped to frame her face and glasses. I noticed that one of her eyelids drooped a little lower than the other, very similar to my grandmother's. And like a grandmother, Sister María Rosa was approachable and huggable and eminently kind: I sensed I could tell her all about my life and she would pay close attention and laugh at the funny parts. Also like a grandmother, she loved to feed visitors. She asked frequently and forcefully in very good English learned during her novitiate in Milwaukee, Wisconsin, if we had enough to eat.

Sister María Rosa posed cheerfully for pictures and chatted with everyone about the previous year's trip, when she had accommodated the whole IHM team around her small television to watch the Indianapolis Colts play in the 2007 Super Bowl. (This was the height of hospitality, because Sister María Rosa's beloved Motagua soccer team was playing on another TV station at the same time.) Suddenly it was time to reboard our bus for an hour's drive to the rural village of Nuevo Paraíso, Sister María Rosa's largest compound of children's homes, where we would stay the week. To my disappointment we had no plans to see her again, yet everyone else seemed perfectly satisfied to have said hello, snapped a photo with her, and then gone our separate ways. Really? I wanted to hear her tell the story of how she started SAN or, more accurately, her outrageous exploits at which my friends had hinted. I was out of luck.

Looking out the bus window at Tegucigalpa, I gaped at corrugated-tin shacks stacked on top of one another, teetering over hilltops in vertical neighborhoods, and wondered where the sewage flows. I saw teenage girls with babies on their hips selling fruit from roadside stands fogged with truck exhaust. In the rain we swerved to avoid a moped pulling onto the highway with three riders piled on, followed by an open pickup truck carrying a wooden coffin and eight soaked family members dressed in funeral finery. As the highway left the city and wound into hills and valleys, I gasped more than once at our driver Armando's calm dexterity as other motorists chose blind mountain curves on which to make triple passes—three vehicles abreast, across the width of the road.

I witnessed human beings living on a razor's edge of danger and destitution, and I remember thinking, *This is like a movie; this can't be real. Is there no justice for these people, no help? How on earth does Sister raise children here?* This was not a world system I could recognize.

When we arrived at Nuevo Paraíso, SAN children came running to greet us with hugs, shouts, paper flowers, and *Bienvenidos* banners of welcome. One special little guy with a shy smile, wearing flip-flops and a too-small Spiderman pajama top, slipped his hand into mine. I felt chosen and loved, even though I thought I was supposed to be the one doing the loving and hugging and giving here.

We settled into the living quarters Sister María Rosa had built for volunteers—very nice beds and bunks with fresh sheets and towels, modern bathrooms, window screens, and even electric fans. I was told that to protest that our dwellings are "too nice" in comparison with the bare-bones children's homes, to show anything less than gratitude, would insult our hosts and their deeply ingrained culture of hospitality. I diligently tried to remember not to put toilet paper into the plumbing and not to brush my teeth with the tap water. (As a group leader today, I carry new toothbrushes with me so we don't have to filch one out of the donations when someone—often it's me—inevitably douses theirs under the tap). At dinner, and at every meal that week, I found the food wonderful and fresh and prepared safely and thoughtfully for American digestive systems: chicken, tilapia, beans, rice, tortillas, fried plantains, papaya, inventive and tasty fruit juices.

In the course of the mission week I sort of forgot about Sister María Rosa. We labored with good intent and great zeal in the naïve hope that our little projects might leave something good and beautiful to offset the ugliness of injustice and poverty. We moved our muscles and chose action over contemplation because it was uncomfortable to pause and think too much about the undeniable and unjust gap between the lives of the rich and those of the poor. We laid brick, shoveled rocks, dispensed vitamins, sorted clothing, mixed paint, planted seeds and bought and bagged food donations for poor families in a nearby village. I ventured footsteps and then leagues out of my comfort zone to do things I'd never consider at home: teeter on a rooftop to paint, attempt with pathetic Spanish a conversation with our Honduran foreman, gyrate awkwardly on the dance floor with teenage girls who swirled like Chita Rivera. I wore myself out and slept soundly through the all-hours ambience of roosters crowing, birds slide-whistling, and the weird native insect that wails like a car alarm.

I made friends with our wonderful hosts and coordinators, who told me stories—some tragic, some triumphant—about the children. I heard how this boy's mother was stabbed to death by his father even as the children lay with her in bed. I heard how another little girl was found alone in her home batting flies away from the body of her mother, who was three days dead. I heard how an indigent grandmother walked for two days to the capital to beg shelter and schooling for her grandkids after a mudslide toppled their rural home into the river. I heard about several of Sister's kids who had become doctors and lawyers.

I began to understand that whatever meager offerings the mission groups bring to help the Honduran people are simply a drop in the bucket of their needs, and that we are actually the ones on the receiving end of gifts—of new intelligence, of meaningful realization that the world operates differently than we thought. I felt restless and fidgety as my heart shifted and my hubris deflated—and would continue to leak air the more times I came to this place—giving my head more space for revelation. We all are poor in so many ways: Sometimes poverty is material and systemic; sometimes it is our understanding that is poor.

On the night before we were to leave, I cried with these parentless kids on whom I had lavished so much attention— the carefree, focused attention I sometimes failed to give my own children being raised with "proper" discipline at home.

I tucked away drawings my new friends had colored for me, along with their notes saying *Dios te bendiga!* (God bless you!) and *Te quiero* (I love you!) I cupped their sweet faces in my hands and in my prayers, and prepared for the reverse culture shock of returning home to the United States.

Then came a marvelous surprise: Sister María Rosa showed up in the dining hall the next morning. She had risen at 3 a.m. for her regular Holy Hour of prayer in her Tegucigalpa chapel, and then ridden out with her driver to Nuevo Paraíso for breakfast with us before our flight. Everyone swarmed around her, but as the newcomer I hung back and watched her easy and familiar relationship with these friends she had known for seven years.

After breakfast, it happened. She sat down and started speaking to the group, telling some of the story of SAN and her life. The room hushed, and her words really did shimmer in the air. She started with her childhood vocation and told colorful highlights of her journey since then.

I wish I could say I was totally enraptured at this first hearing of her story, but I was in a predicament: My backpack with trusty notebook and pen was out of reach on a table across the room. This was a problem because Sister María Rosa is extremely quotable. She was spouting beautiful epithets I wanted desperately to write down, but no one else moved, so I froze, too. I was reduced to trying to memorize choice lines with mnemonic devices. It worked, because I still remember a couple of odd ones today, like "IS MY WIG" ("If I Start with MoneY, Where Is God?").

After an hour, Sister María Rosa concluded, wished us well, and returned to Tegucigalpa. I grabbed my backpack and notebook and bolted for the bus, trying not to hear any other words that might displace the nuggets crammed in my head. I spilled out on paper everything I could remember she said, starting with this motto: "The dignity of life is to work, not to beg."

Sister María Rosa with the author in 2009 and 2019

CHAPTER 1

IN HOT PURSUIT

SISTER MARÍA ROSA LITERALLY CHASES HER DREAM OF PROVIDING A HOPEFUL FUTURE TO ABANDONED CHILDREN

--"Children have the right to be happy.
So God sent me to help them."--

In Tegucigalpa, the capital city of Honduras, in 1966, a short, plump, middle-aged Catholic nun was hot on the heels of the richest man in the country. Sister María Rosa Leggol, a hospital nurse with a fifth-grade education, had no money, no social standing, no clout. What she did have was the audacity to ask big favors of powerful men and the unwavering conviction that her dream—to rescue, house, and educate street children—was sanctioned by God.

She also had the gall to think she could stop the man's airplane from taking off.

Sister María Rosa needed this man, a board member of her new child rescue project Sociedad Amigos de los Niños (SAN), to sign the mortgage for one of ten brand-new buildings she had commissioned from a local builder to house at-risk children.

"I ordered those ten homes, but I didn't know I had to pay for them," Sister María Rosa laughed when she told this story decades later. "I thought if I came to a big building company and said that I needed homes for poor children, they would just give it to me!"

She needed all of SAN's board members—wealthy businesspeople, media owners, and lawyers, the "movers and shakers" of Tegucigalpa—to pledge to contribute, but these friends in high places were unlikely to be found in their offices when she wanted something from them. This last man whose signature Sister María Rosa needed had slipped her grasp for weeks. Arriving by taxi that day at his home, she was told he was at the airport, about to jet off on a lengthy business trip.

"I could never find that guy, because businessmen spend more time on the plane than at home!" Sister María Rosa exclaimed, exasperated. "But this was the last day before the signatures were due, so I ran back to the taxi and asked the driver to drive me fast to the airport!"

When her taxi arrived at Toncontin Airport, Sister María Rosa hurried to the Departures desk. The agent informed her that all the passengers—including her board member—were already seated on the flight, the plane's door was closed, and the pilot was ready for takeoff. She told the nun to turn around and go home.

Instead, Sister María Rosa took off running through the airport. Before any security guards could stop her, she plunged out a door onto the tarmac. There was a single DC-3 in motion, starting to taxi toward the airport's lone asphalt runway. Out of breath, Sister María Rosa galloped toward the front of the jet, jumping and waving wildly at the pilot's window, yelling, "Stop the plane!"

Incredibly, the plane slowed to a halt. As Sister María Rosa caught her breath, a flight attendant opened the door to the plane and lowered a stairway. Sister María Rosa hurried up into the plane, brandishing her mortgage papers and shouting the businessman's name. The astonished man came forward and signed them. Later he said, "Who can say no to Sister María Rosa?"

"He didn't even ask me what he was signing, so I gave him the papers for *two* homes," Sister María Rosa chuckled. "Then I said thank you to the pilot and goodbye to everyone else. When I turned around to go down the stairs, there were policemen yelling at me, 'You are not supposed to be there!' So I thought quickly, then I turned around and blessed the plane with my arms in a big sign of the cross and told the people, 'Here is the blessing I came to give you for your journey!' After that I ran past the policemen to the taxi and we got out of there!"

As providence would have it, the pilot stopped the plane because he actually recognized Sister María Rosa down on the tarmac. Weeks earlier, his wife had delivered a baby at Tegucigalpa's La Policlínica hospital, and Sister María Rosa had been her nurse.

"Can you see how God plans everything?" Sister María Rosa concluded. "Why did that pilot know me and stop the plane? Why did the man come forth and sign the papers for my homes? So that on the day they were due, all my mortgage and grant papers were signed and at the American Embassy! This was all in God's plan.

"Money to start my project with? What is money to me?" she continued—a prophetic statement for her organization's frequent financial struggles. "If I start with money, then where is God?"

***

THIS IS THE STORY OF AN ORPHAN WHO BECAME *MADRE*, Mother, to tens of thousands of children in the second-poorest country in the Western Hemisphere. It is the tale of a social entrepreneur who gave abandoned kids a chance to stay safely in Honduras rather than flee its poverty, violence, and lax child labor laws only to end up caged as unaccompanied minors at the U.S. border. This is also the saga of a humble Franciscan nun slinging her iron will and trust in God, like David versus Goliath, at the enormous Third World power disparity between the poor and the rich, women and men, the anonymous and the well connected.

The life story of Sister María Rosa, who died in 2020 at age 93 and whose cause for sainthood is already being promoted, is extraordinary and improbable, especially given its setting. Honduras is known for its endemic corruption, political unrest, weak law enforcement, natural disasters, machismo culture, and gang violence on a scale most North Americans cannot fathom. Two-thirds of the country's population of nearly ten million live in poverty. A quarter of Hondurans drop out of school after sixth grade. Unemployment is perennially high. Child prostitution and sexual exploitation are rampant, and severe gang violence has earned Honduras the titles of Murder Capital of the World and Most Violent Nation Not at War.

The country's challenges today—and its desperate need for Sister María Rosa's vision and mission—are not so different from those it faced in 1966, when Sister María Rosa yearned simply to give homeless street kids a safe place to live. From the windows of her workplace as a nurse at La Policlínica, she saw abandoned children sleeping under newspapers in alleys or curled up inside cardboard boxes under city bridges. She witnessed young kids begging on street corners (many under the command of adults), rummaging through garbage for food scraps, and huffing glue to quell hunger pains. She worried about the children locked up inside squalid prison cells with their incarcerated mothers or fathers, as was the custom in Honduras until the 1990s.

No reliable government or social programs existed for these children; there was no safety net. So Sister María Rosa founded her own child-rescue program, SAN, against all odds, with no startup funding and no promise of financial support from her religious order. All she had was a strong notion that was revolutionary at the time: to shelter children in small-group homes with housemothers, rather than large institutional orphanages. She would raise them in "families," where each child would enjoy safety, education, and health, plus the individual attention and love needed to grow into a good man or woman.

"To take in children you have to work with whatever problem they have," she said. "You need to change their lives, not just the place where they live. You have to take care of all that love the children have been missing since they were conceived."

In the beginning her project was fairly small and straight-forward: Sister María Rosa built ten little houses that would become safe, loving homes where abandoned and trauma-tized kids could live and heal and grow. Then she marched into Tegucigalpa's Central Penitentiary, brought out the children living in cells with imprisoned parents, and placed them in the first home. As word spread about "the nun who helps children," her houses quickly overflowed with young people in dire straits. So she built more homes. And then schools. And then vocational programs. Out of those humble seeds, some incredible turns of events, and perhaps a little divine intervention bloomed a national network of children's villages, schools, farms, clinics, training centers, and microbusinesses, all dedicated to helping Sister María Rosa's children grow up to become productive working adults and contributors to their families and communities.

Today SAN encompasses diverse social projects for the most vulnerable children and families in Honduras. The organization is often mistaken for an "orphanage," but most SAN kids are not exactly orphans in the legal sense of having no parents. Sister María Rosa expanded the definition of "orphan" to a reality more native to Honduras: economic orphans, moral orphans, orphans in principle—children unloved, abused, abandoned, neglected, or forsaken by grownups. They are children who saw their father kill their mother in a drunken rage. They are toddlers who were incarcerated with their drug-dealer mothers in coed prison cells without security, stimulation, or socialization, sleeping under their mother's bodies to keep from being molested. They are young boys and girls whose parents left them to work in the United States and never came back. They are city kids, homeless and starving, who darted out into traffic to wash car windows and beg for payment, easily targeted by gangs. They are rural kids who had to walk two hours each way to and from school on remote trails marked by dangerous river crossings and predatory men. Most of all, they are children who without Sister María Rosa's help would likely be forced to flee Honduras's poverty and violence, hunger and hardship for the deadly trek north through Guatemala and Mexico toward the U.S. border.

The desperation of children and families to escape Honduras is manifest today in the surging numbers of unaccompanied Central American minors arriving continuously at the southern U.S. border. In fiscal year 2012, 13,000 kids—mostly from the Northern Triangle countries of Honduras, Guatemala, and El Salvador—were referred to the U.S. Office of Refugee Resettlement by the Department of Homeland Security. In 2013 there were 25,000 referrals; in 2014, 57,000; and in 2019, 70,000. In the single month of March 2021, nearly 19,000 unaccompanied children were detained at the border—double the number of kids caught in February 2021, according to the U.S. Customs and Border Protection agency. In 2020, 65 percent of these children were younger than 17, and about 15 percent of those were ages 6 to 12.

Most of the Honduran teens, children, and families are fleeing not just poverty but gang violence. A recent United Nations High Commissioner for Refugees report showed that an incredible 44 percent of the Honduran children interviewed at the U.S. border had been directly threatened or victimized by gangs. In Honduras, even very young children are targeted and strong-armed into serving as messengers or lookouts during gang crimes. Older kids are often recruited directly into drug trafficking, robbery, extortion, and murder. Refusal to join the MS-13 or Barrio 18 gangs can result in the kidnapping, rape, or killing of relatives and friends. Gang recruitment is downright easy at times: Vulnerable kids whose families have disintegrated are often initially attracted to older gang members who serve as substitute parents.

Sister María Rosa's kids, on the other hand, have no need to flee their home country. Her 50 determined years in this challenging arena have provided desperately poor children safety, education and job training *right in Honduras*. SAN has a long and laudable track record, its grown children contributing to the Honduran economy today as business managers and owners, teachers and professors, directors of medical clinics, furniture designers, computer repair specialists, and international consultants. One is a staff member in the Honduran Congress. Several have earned scholarships to study in the United States and Europe. Many work in some capacity for SAN, as cooks, accountants, and program directors, striving to give back to the nun who raised them. Their own children go to university now, disrupting the legacy of unemployment and exponentially improving Honduran lives.

❦

IN ITS HALF-CENTURY OF EMPOWERING AT-RISK CHILDREN, SAN has also empowered thousands of North American and European mission travelers who arrive on its doorstep, duffels of donations in hand, unsure of what to do, say, or even think. Mission volunteers can be like children in need, too—green and inexperienced in an unfamiliar culture and language, often dumbfounded at witnessing real-life poverty up close. Travel, with its twin rucksacks of disorientation and discomfort, is prime breeding ground for transformation, which Sister María Rosa cannily facilitated as she welcomed mission teams over that threshold where rich and poor, familiar and foreign, meet. Her influence on these visitors was crucial to SAN's long-term success.

"When you go to heaven you will see you were in God's

book to be here with us," she liked to tell the mission teams, her eyes brightening above her characteristic open-mouthed grin. "You'll see that you had an appointment with us made in heaven back in 1966 when I started. He is happy you are finally here!"

With that unflinching faith in God's larger plan, Sister María Rosa guided her mission groups to simple *be with* the children and Honduran adults, rather than try, with North American fervor and can-do ingenuity, to fix poverty or restore lives. She told them that she was grateful for the donations, the school backpack collections, child sponsorship drives, and gala fundraisers, but that the most important gift was relationship with her people and with the children who she said "are becoming a new generation with hope as they learn to love again!"

Sister María Rosa was always good at asking for help and collaboration—and so she got it. She invited mission groups to get to know her children, instructed them to come back often, and then made bold and crucial requests of their time and resources. Holding nothing back, not even the traumatic histories of her kids' lives, Sister María Rosa nurtured intimate long-term family relationships with the mission teams, who feel compelled to return year after year. (I have traveled to work at her mission nearly 30 times since 2008.)

Many visitors who respond to Sister María Rosa's invitation are drawn irresistibly into SAN's projects and its children. Their lives are upended, leaving them to wonder: How did this humble but willful nun transform a one-week mission trip into a lifelong pursuit that feels imperative, like work they are meant to do, like God's plan? Where did she get the vision, charisma, and moxie to knock people off the tracks of their own life course and redirect them toward helping poor children in Honduras?

Sister María Rosa herself was never concerned with an answer to that question. All of the help from the groups was simply a wonderful outcome for which she claimed no credit or responsibility. To her, this was all in God's divine plan.

"María Rosa did not and could not do all this. I am just one woman," she declared. "But María Rosa and God...? You'd be surprised what we can do!"

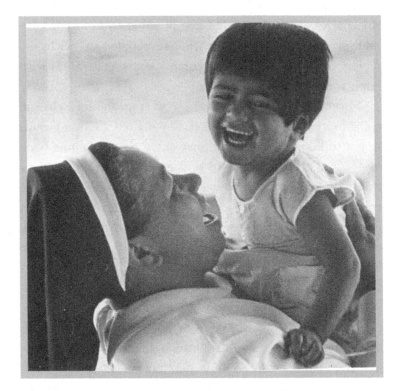

CHAPTER 2

AN EARLY VOCATION

SISTER MARÍA ROSA'S DEVOTION TO
ORPHANS BEGINS AT THE TENDER AGE
OF SIX

*--"If we believe in what we are doing—if we are exactly clear that
the Lord is there in our work, helping us, giving us the strength we
need, there will never be a problem. Love and faith can do anything
in the world."--*

I t takes an orphan to know one. This is how Sister
María Rosa Leggol's story starts. Abandonment by her
father and the death of her mother set her on a path
she was certain God laid deliberately, stone by stone,
uniquely for her. Her mission to rescue children and shelter
orphans was absolutely home-grown. Only another orphan
could truly comprehend the deep hole and endless ache for
personal attention in the lives of children without parents.

Maria Rosa Leggol was born November 21, 1926, in El
Paraíso, outside the bustling port town of Puerto Cortés on
the northwest coast of Honduras. Founded in 1524, Puerto
Cortés was originally named Puerto de Caballos, Port of

Horses, for the animals that drowned as Spanish explorer Hernan Cortés unloaded them from his ships. The town became Puerto Cortés in 1869, when railway construction inland to Potrerillos began, and by the time Sister María Rosa was born it was a company town for the banana industry. The United Fruit Company, later known as Chiquita Brands International, and the Standard Fruit Company, which became Dole Foods, employed nearly everyone in the region. Bananas comprised upward of 80 percent of Honduras's exports, and these rival companies embroiled themselves in every facet of Honduran politics and economics, bolstered by U.S. protection where necessary.

María Rosa was the youngest of four girls born to Irene Rosales. Her father, Josef Le-gol or Leggol, was a French Canadian merchant marine from Halifax, Nova Scotia, who originally came to Honduras to "bring back the bananas," she said. He left the family before she was a year old. Irene tried to keep her daughters together, but she worked long days as a cook and housekeeper, so she sent her youngest child at age four to live with her godparents. María Rosa stayed overnight with her mother and sisters infrequently. Every one of them worked, including her sisters Norma, Emma, and Paula (short for Leopoldina), who cleaned rental houses near the beach and cooked for parties in the homes of the wealthy.

"My sisters would go to school a little and work a little," said Sister María Rosa, who attended school through the fifth grade. "We all worked big jobs, jobs for people older than us. It was not an easy life."

From age six, María Rosa labored cooking coconut bread and tortillas and selling them on the streets of Puerto Cortés. She started very early in the morning, peddling them in people's kitchens or to plantation employees on their way to work. María Rosa was an enterprising child, and a quick breakfast was an easy sell. (This salesmanship experience would serve her well in all the SAN microbusinesses she would launch in the future.)

"Since my godparents were taking care of me, it was my job to help them with some money," she said. "Then I would go to school by 7 a.m. We had to be there by 7 or the door would be closed. Just one time I was one minute late. But the teacher opened the door for me because I had always been on time, even though I was working in the morning."

María Rosa attended school from 7 to 11 a.m. and 2 to 5 p.m., with a one-hour study period at the end of the day. "There were no books, but you could stay and ask the teacher questions," she remembered. "We learned things like calligraphy and writing clearly. Then on Saturdays we went to school from 7 to 10 a.m. and they taught us important things to respect, like our country's flag, symbols and songs."

A high school education was not in the cards for María Rosa. At that time, most schools in Honduras didn't go beyond sixth grade. The country's few high schools were in the large cities of Tegucigalpa and San Pedro Sula; some wealthy children went all the way to the Jesuit high school in neighboring Belize. In fact, most of María Rosa's teachers had only seven years of education—just two more than María Rosa would have.

Into this busy childhood of hard work and long school-days came a very early calling to religious life. For María Rosa, it was no gentle or slow realization, no gradual unfolding of a delicate rose. Instead, her vocation barreled down on her, dressed in flowing black robes with "little pink faces, like apples, sticking out."

"I remember the day exactly, because it was my sixth birthday," she said. "I saw religious Sisters at the port, coming off a ship. I had never seen them before and couldn't understand why they wore all black, why they dressed like that in the heat. So I asked our priest why they were all wrapped up that way. He explained that there are girls and women in the world who devote their lives to helping children, orphans, and sick people, that they work in places like hospitals and orphanages. He told me the whole thing! I wasn't an orphan yet myself, but I had two friends at school who had no parents and were mistreated badly. I felt sorry for them and wanted to help them. So I decided, if these Sisters work to help orphans I want to be one of them!"

The nuns were members of the order of School Sisters of Saint Francis from Baden, in southwestern Germany. They were passing through Puerto Cortés on their way to the interior of Honduras and were gone almost as soon as they arrived. María Rosa didn't know where they went or how she would find them again. When she told the priest that she wanted to join the nuns, he laughed at her young age and told her to put the crazy idea out of her head. Still, the notion of religious life took very firm hold. As a young child, María Rosa attended church and faithfully celebrated the sacraments, even if she had to do it alone. "I made my First Communion at six years of age without anyone's permission, wearing my mother's wedding dress," she once told a Tegucigalpa newspaper reporter.

Though María Rosa lived with her godparents, she passed by the house of her mother and older sisters on her way to school. One morning when María Rosa was around seven or eight years old, Irene felt very ill and asked her youngest daughter to run to the pharmacy to bring back some kind of seltzer. The store was far away, and by the time the girl returned, her mother had died.

Sister María Rosa remembered several things about her mother: She had a beautiful singing voice (which Sister María Rosa inherited), played the violin, and was a wonderful cook. Sister María Rosa also recalled her mother's devotion to prayer.

"When I was visiting her and there was a hurricane or storm or bad weather she would wake us girls in the middle of the night and tell us we had to come pray," she said. "When we lived near the shore in Cortés we would pray for those people out on the boats, out on the ocean. We prayed to the Blessed Mother with our little arms stretched out for a long time. My mother was a very simple lady, but she had a lot of faith. When I ask myself now why I pray so much, it is because that's what my family did."

Another legacy of Irene's faith was her strong devotion to the poor. She raised her daughters with an expectation that they would serve others. When Sister María Rosa was growing up, she says, the poor were allowed to beg only on Saturday. They would come by train from the smaller towns and villages to Puerto Cortés to ask for help.

"My mother told us girls, 'You eat from Sunday through Friday, but on Saturday you will cook for the poor,'" Sister María Rosa recounted. "So we would cook food and go to the train to serve the poor people and give them water to drink and to wash with. I thought everybody was doing the same thing. I thought the whole world treated the poor just like that."

After Irene's death, the family disintegrated. Norma, Emma, and Paula moved away to work in houses where they could also live. María Rosa felt abandoned anew when none of them could take their little sister with them. That fresh stab of rejection pushed her straight into the arms of another mother: Mary, the Mother of God. Even as a young child, she considered the Blessed Mother a close friend and confidante.

"I knew that the Blessed Mother went through a lot at a very young age, too," Sister María Rosa said. "She was a nice little girl who said yes to the Holy Spirit, but she had a hard time. She was a teenage mother with no place to have a baby except a dirty barn filled with animals. And it was so cold and there was nothing to put on the baby. But God showed Mary how to go through, how to have faith, be humble, and trust that everything would be OK because God was right there, going through all that with her. So I knew, even when I was young, that He was there with me in my troubles.

"My friends and I who had no parents would say to each other, 'Oh, we are not orphans. We have the Blessed Mother, and she is our mother.' This is a strong thing for a young child to say and feel. And that's the way my vocation developed—very strongly."

Around age nine, María Rosa started thinking again about those Sisters who worked with orphans. She was getting older; was it time to find the Sisters and become one of them? She went to church and prayed, *Blessed Mother, where are those Sisters I saw from years ago? How can I find them? If you don't help me to find them, how can I help the orphans?*

Her prayer was answered in minutes. When she walked out of the church, she saw a boat arrive in the harbor. Off that boat stepped two nuns, School Sisters of Saint Francis from Germany on their way to staff an orphanage in Comayagua, two hours inland.

María Rosa strode boldly up to the nuns and insisted on

accompanying them, wherever they were going. They told her they would be taking the train to Comayagua in two days, probably assuming the little girl would forget or change her mind.

"I kept the secret for two days," Sister María Rosa remembered. "I didn't tell my godparents, because I thought if they told me no and I went anyway, I would be disobeying. I didn't want to disobey, ever. This way, I thought I wasn't disobeying."

Two days later she sneaked onto the train and left Puerto Cortés. At first she wasn't missed at home because it was a Sunday and her godparents assumed she was at Mass as usual. She said she had to hide every time the conductor came around because she had no money for a ticket. He must have seen her, however, because back in Puerto Cortés later that day, the conductor told María Rosa's godfather, who was looking for her, where she had gone.

"So my godfather said, 'Oh, she finally did it. She always said that was what she wanted to do—go with the Sisters,'" Sister María Rosa said. "They sent me word that I could come back if I wanted. But I never did go back."

When the train reached Comayagua, María Rosa got off and presented herself—"Here I am!"—to the surprised nuns. She went with them to their large orphanage and remained there for the rest of her childhood. She lived with the nuns and 260 other girls, waiting, as she put it, "to grow *rapidito*, become a nun, and go pick up my children." She was a quick study, watching the Sisters care for so many children at once.

"I played like I was a nurse or doctor, taking care of all the kids," she said. "I was very observant all the time and I wanted to learn exactly what to do with children who don't have a home; I was still thinking of my two friends from school. I was always interested in what's going on with that child who didn't look happy or didn't feel good. I spent those first years finding out what to do with them, what they like, what they don't, why they are sad."

A dream began to take concrete shape in María Rosa's head. She started imagining the children's homes she would create when she grew up. They bore little resemblance to the one in which she lived, which she deemed too big to give the personal, individual attention every child needed. She said she used to nag the Sisters, "Why don't you eat with us at our tables if you are our mothers? And why do we have to sleep together, so many in one space?" María Rosa decided that *her* orphanage would consist of many separate small homes so that every child would be part of a family, with brothers and sisters, a regular kitchen table, and regular bedrooms.

She also decided after several years that it was time to move on, to take the next step toward her dream of becoming a nun. She wanted to go work with the School Sisters who were nurses in Tegucigalpa.

"I knew how to cook and clean and take care of children without parents already," said Sister María Rosa. "So I began bothering the Sisters to send me to Tegucigalpa to learn what to do with sick people." Then she confided with a smile, "Back then, I thought I had to do everything the nuns did, in order: care for orphans, then help the sick. I bothered them so much they finally sent me."

At a young age, María Rosa entrenched herself in certainty that God had a blueprint for her life and that she would follow it. Every step she would take would be guided by His plan.

"All my life since I was very young, I know that the Lord

has been asking me to do something. I just keep trying to hear and understand Him," she said. "Even from age six in my young small mind God was already present. Otherwise I couldn't have discerned this vocation.

"I am a simple woman; I have never had too much of anything. I speak the language of the poor and the abandoned. They understand me. The Lord is always speaking the language of the poor, so I understand Him, too."

María Rosa as a teenager

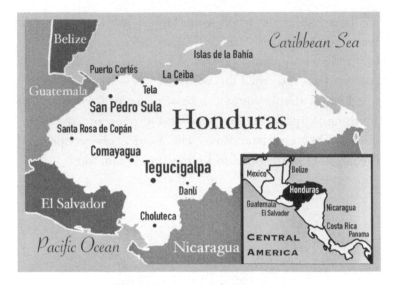

German School Sisters of Saint Francis in Honduras in the 1930s

CHAPTER 3

RELIGIOUS FORMATION

SISTER MARÍA ROSA JOINS THE SCHOOL SISTERS OF SAINT FRANCIS IN MILWAUKEE, WISCONSIN

--"Never wait until somebody says 'do.'
Go ahead and do what you find in the way."--

A t age 14, María Rosa moved to Tegucigalpa to live and work with the nuns who were hospital nurses at La Policlínica. Here she learned to pray every morning with the Sisters. (The early prayer time was a habit she kept all her life, rising at three for her Holy Hour in her Tegucigalpa chapel before attending Mass at four, said daily by her friend Father Max Velásquez.) As a teenager, she especially loved learning prayers in Latin.

"Latin for me is like a way to speak with God," she said. "Latin has no words to insult. It must be God's language."

Because she had no nursing training, María Rosa was initially relegated to La Policlínica's X-ray department, where she developed the images.

"There was a very nice doctor who taught me the job and

how to work with the plates," she said. "But I didn't like spending all day alone in that dark room. I wanted to see people, be with people."

Next the Sisters sent her to the lab, where she learned how to process tests, but again spent her days alone, as she described, "counting red cells and white cells." So for the first of many times in her life, she identified a need and made up her own job. When she noticed that the Sisters had to climb up and down four floors in the hospital all day and night, she asked her Superior if she could help them at night, after her lab job, to "be their legs and go up and down the floors when they needed something."

So María Rosa became a "gopher" for the night nurses. She didn't know the names of medical instruments or equipment, so the nurses would draw a picture of what they wanted her to get. She learned quickly from the hospital staff—not just the names of things, but what the doctors and nurses and patients needed in general. Soon she could predict what they would ask for and have it ready.

"I didn't realize that it was a big help and I didn't know how much I was learning about nursing," she said. "I was just happy to finally be working with people."

María Rosa spent eight formative years living and working with the nursing Sisters until, at age 22, she finally fulfilled a goal she had set at age six. She was accepted into the religious community of her caretakers and started the formal process to become a School Sister of Saint Francis.

At this point in her story, Sister María Rosa always stopped and invoked divine providence.

"Do you see how nothing just happens in life?" she asked. "It's all God's plan. God's plan has been with me since I was born. So many things happened: Why did my father leave and my mother die? Why did those nuns come all the way from Germany to my hometown on my birthday? God wanted them to find me and me to find them!"

"God's plan" was pretty much a mantra with Sister María Rosa. She spoke of God's plan with the same familiarity the rest of us take with our daily to-do list. For most of us, it's hard to recognize single steps as part of a grand plan while they are actually happening. Sometimes we're lucky enough to look at our lives in retrospect and notice that the character-building moments and important decisions stand out like bright red poppies in a garden mosaic we can't decipher until we step back and squint our eyes a little. María Rosa, however, at age six latched onto God's plan for her and embraced it with the fervor of the child she was, with zeal and a dogged stubbornness that would sustain her on a very rugged path.

On June 13, 1949, in Milwaukee, Wisconsin, María Rosa began her formation as a School Sister of Saint Francis. Most girls spent a year of inquiry at the convent before committing to the order, but María Rosa was already 22 rather than 15 or 16, like the other arrivals. So she was fast-tracked. She had been with the Sisters since childhood anyway, first in the orphanage, then working with them at La Policlínica.

Because the School Sisters in Honduras had come originally from Germany, Sister María Rosa said she should have been sent to Germany for her religious training. In the late 1940s, though, Germany was still unsettled from the ravages of World War II. The Sisters sent María Rosa and the other Latin American girls instead to their American province in Milwaukee.

This Wisconsin branch, founded in 1874 by three School Sisters from a small community in Schwarzach, Germany, had established schools and hospitals throughout the United States. They had begun serving in Latin America in the 1930s, a decade or more after their European counterparts. As a Franciscan order, the School Sisters' mission is to witness to the presence of Jesus on earth by entering into the lives of the poor all around the world. Their work is guided by values of prayer, poverty, and "minority"—seeking out poor and marginalized people and living in solidarity among them. Sister María Rosa was a natural at this one.

Today the School Sisters of Saint Francis number more than 600 women who teach, nurse, and serve the poor in the United States, Latin America, Europe, and India. When María Rosa arrived in 1949, however, there were more than 500 Sisters in Milwaukee alone.

María Rosa found the quiet, tree-lined campus in the American Midwest "majestic," she said, compared with the grit and noise of Tegucigalpa. On Milwaukee's historic South Layton Boulevard, the stately Saint Joseph motherhouse was the original site of Alverno College, chartered by the Sisters in 1887; it is one of the largest four-year Catholic women's colleges in the nation today. The building in María Rosa's time was constructed in 1891 to replace the original convent lost in a fire. The School Sisters' Italian Romanesque–style Saint Joseph Chapel was for María Rosa a magnificent place for prayer; she'd never seen anything like it. Its 115 stained glass windows were crafted in Innsbruck, Austria, and every nook in the walls, altar, and floor was inlaid with intricate mosaic stones—artwork that María Rosa and her classmates used to scrub daily on their hands and knees.

Like many of the girls arriving from Latin America for formation, María Rosa knew not a word of English when she arrived. She had instead picked up a lot of German while living with the nuns in Comayagua. ("I would sing the Mass in German with them, not even knowing what I was saying," she remembered.) She took some English lessons with a Spanish teacher at Alverno College, but most of her excellent English today came simply from immersion during her two years in Milwaukee.

"That's why I feel sorry for the ones who come to Honduras today to help us with our work here and can't speak Spanish," she said. "Back then I thought I didn't have time to sit in a classroom and learn English. All I knew was that I wanted to become a Sister, so I could come back to Honduras and help the children without parents."

"Those poor girls from Latin America!" remembered Sister Kathlyn Brenner, mission advancement volunteer and former director of the School Sisters of Saint Francis. She was Sister María Rosa's close friend since their days together as novices. "Decades later we started doing formation in the young women's countries of origin, but in the late forties, they came here. So many of them didn't know English; some had never even worn shoes before. They were struggling just to walk, clomping around in uncomfortable shoes. The food was so different to them; there was just nothing familiar. You could walk in the garden with them, but we'd have nothing to say because we couldn't understand each other's language. Back then, we weren't supposed to be talking anyway!"

Still, María Rosa was resourceful at figuring out what was going on. "One thing that helped me was that in our community every group wore a different dress," she noted. "I was a postulant at first and had a little black veil so I followed around the people with the black veils. Then in my novitiate my veil was white so I followed the white veils. I laughed when everybody laughed and I was serious when everyone was serious; I just did whatever everybody around me was doing. They didn't even realize that I didn't understand too much of it."

Sister María Rosa recalled two funny stories about her language barrier. "One day it was snowing very hard," she said. "I had never seen that before, and I just couldn't come in out of the snow for class. So the Mother Superior had to come outside with some Sisters to find me. Those Sisters told me later that after she found me she was scolding me and telling me that I was not obedient, but I had no idea what she was saying. I couldn't think of the words to apologize and she was waiting for an answer, so what came out of my mouth was, 'I wish you the same, Mother.' Thank goodness she laughed at that!"

The other story had to do with the Sisters trying to teach her the name of an insect flying around the kitchen. They said, "Look, María Rosa. This is a ladybug!" And María Rosa replied shrewdly, "How do you know that this one is a lady?"

She spent a lot of time helping in the kitchen or the laundry and working in the cellar because she didn't need English to tackle those chores. "I was happy to go and do something instead of sitting and listening in a lot of meetings that told us what to do and what not to do," she said. The work in the cellar was infamous among Sister María Rosa's classmates, who called themselves "the 49ers" for the year they entered the novitiate and "rebels" because they took Saint Joan of Arc as their role model. They remembered chanting, "Keep your eyes on your hands and your hands on your work," as they scrubbed potatoes, dug for worms in the dirt of the cellar floor, and tried to keep beet juice from splashing their white veils.

Her fellow 49ers remembered María Rosa as "very fun"—

lively and friendly and engaging, even before she learned English. They also called her a delight and a free thinker.

"She was such a free spirit," said Brenner. "Many of the other Latin girls were very submissive and quiet. She arrived in Milwaukee in an age of 'Yes, Sister' and 'No, Sister'; that was how we spoke. But not María Rosa. Some of it was that she didn't understand the language at first, but some of it was just her personality—even at that young age. She would ask questions no one else would dare ask!"

"She was a spitfire," said Sister Joan Wilde, another 49er who lives in a suburb of Milwaukee. "She was 20 years ahead of her time. We were such a closed community then."

Sister María Rosa treasured her time in Milwaukee, which gave her a new notion of family. "I felt like I was in heaven there because the community was so beautiful, with so many holy Sisters and buses full of young girls coming into the community every year," she said. "I loved all the singing and the prayers together. I loved our perpetual adoration chapel, too—I used to take the hour from 1 a.m. to 2 a.m. because I never did sleep much.

"My community for me is such a great thing. I didn't have anyone and the Lord was so good to bring me to a big family. There are not too many families like that in the world, and when I began this work with the children in Honduras I told everybody we have to make a big family and help each other."

🙣

MARÍA ROSA LEFT MILWAUKEE AS A SISTER RIGHT AFTER professing first, or temporary, vows in 1951. She returned eagerly to Tegucigalpa, relieved to be done with training.

"I'm not a person who has too much patience to sit in a classroom when somebody is out there sick or dying and needs me," she concluded.

She went back to work at La Policlínica as a night nurse while planning and waiting for her opportunity to create homes for poor children. In the capital city she encountered abandoned, impoverished, and abused kids everywhere. They begged for food on street corners and slept under newspapers in the alleys or beneath the arcades of crumbling buildings. Working the night shift had advantages: Sister María Rosa could sneak food and blankets out of the hospital to give them.

While her mission for abandoned children felt urgent and necessary, Sister María Rosa knew the timing wasn't right to ask her community for permission to leave the hospital and start a new venture. "They told me that no Sister could go alone," she said. "Sisters had to work and live in twos or threes or more. They said I was fine to stay working in La Policlínica."

So Sister María Rosa accepted the fact that she must wait to fulfill her true vocation. "I believe you have to teach your-self how to live, accommodate yourself to whatever is going on where you are, and don't let anybody think you are sad or lost," she said. "You make your own life, wherever you are."

Besides, she wasn't sure she had the experience to start such a daunting project. "God has a special time, hour, and minute for us," she continued. "That was not my time. I still had to be blessed to do the work with children."

Meanwhile, Sister María Rosa made the most of her time in nursing. She says she loved the patients and enjoyed visiting them at night, singing to them, rubbing their backs, freshening their pillows. People at the hospital liked Sister

María Rosa very much; she made friends with wealthy families she would later call on to support her project. One invaluable contact became Sister María Rosa's close friend and a cofounder of SAN: Reyes Irene Valenzuela, a businesswoman with good contacts in the community and churches who knew how to get things done in Tegucigalpa.

"Reyes was a woman of the world, but she was very good, very positive, not like some other women in business," Sister María Rosa remembered. "She prayed all the time; we used to pray the rosary together. She taught me how to play canasta. She was my friend outside the Sisters. And when she was not working with banks and companies, she was helping me to start Sociedad Amigos de los Niños, telling me what to do and say, watching so I wouldn't do anything that was wrong."

Reyes's sister, Valerie, took on a special project with Sister María Rosa: caring for the baby of a sick mother who had gone blind during pregnancy. The baby had started crawling and the mother couldn't keep him safe; she had to tether his wrist or ankle to the bed so he wouldn't wander off. Sister María Rosa promised the mother that she would take care of the child herself. Valerie watched the baby during the day and Sister María Rosa during her night shift at La Policlínica.

"The baby's name was Marco Antonio," Sister María Rosa noted. "I didn't want to tell the Sisters that I had the baby; I didn't have permission. My thinking at the time was: If I ask permission, they might say no."

The baby's mother soon died. Sister María Rosa continued to care for Marco Antonio, her first child, before SAN was even founded. Reyes and Valerie Valenzuela helped Sister María Rosa run a coffee and food shop next to the hospital to earn money for the boy's little clothes and diapers. They also worked for seed money to eventually start Sister María Rosa's children's homes. They called it Cafeteria Por Niños Sin Hogar—for children without homes. Sister María Rosa baked the muffins and rolls and cookies at night in the hospital kitchen to provide the next day's stock.

"I would pinch food from the kitchen at the hospital to make a few things to sell the next day," she said. "I already had a reputation for handing out medicines to the poor for free and taking hospital blankets out to the people sleeping on the streets. It was stealing, yes, but at the time I thought I was doing something helpful: I was helping the hospital to give something up for the poor.

"This was my own thinking, not anybody else's, though!" she was quick to add.

Eventually, when the first Americans began to arrive in Honduras to volunteer in SAN's children's homes, a young woman took Marco Antonio home with her to Michigan to have eye surgery. He was losing his sight, like his mother. After months of eye operations, he was adopted and raised by a couple in Michigan.

Months at the coffee shop and years in the hospital helped acquaint Sister María Rosa with many Tegucigalpa businessmen and professionals. "I called all these people my friends and later made them my first board of directors when I founded Sociedad Amigos de los Niños," she said with pride. SAN's first board president, Don Pedro Atala Simón, an influential Tegucigalpa businessman, first met Sister María Rosa during a family emergency and later joined her board of directors because of it.

"I didn't remember this," Sister María Rosa told the story, "but he says that one night he came running into La

Policlínica because his cousin had a bad accident and was in a smaller hospital where there was no blood. I worked in the lab and knew how to make the bag that they needed, so I fixed it for him. I told him to take it quickly to his cousin and I would get another one ready for him when he came back. I told him he would need two or three. When he came back he told me that the doctors said the bag was prepared exactly right for giving it in a special way when someone has no blood pressure and that he did need two more. I had them ready for him. And then he wanted to pay but didn't have his wallet in all the commotion. I told him to just run with the blood to his cousin and pay another day, which he did. So years later, when I called the businessmen to ask if they might help me in my work with the children, he said, 'Of course I will. I want to help you in the same way you helped me.' And he came onto my board of directors and helped us for many, many years. I tell you, you just don't know these things while they are happening."

Sister María Rosa (third from right) greets other Sisters

MADRE

PROFILE: THE COLLEGE VOLUNTEER WHO BECAME A HEALTHCARE CEO FOR MIGRANTS

Bobbi McIvor Ryder

Bobbi McIvor Ryder was the first North American volunteer whose life was radically altered by experiences with Sister María Rosa. She was only 18 when she came to Honduras on a break from college; she was the young woman who took Sister María Rosa's first baby, Marco Antonio, home to the United States for the eye operations he needed. More than 50 years later, she recently retired as CEO of the National Center for Farmworker Health, a not-for-profit corporation in Buda, Texas, that provides information and training to migrant health centers around the United States. Most of her work was with Central American immigrants to the country, including many from Honduras.

"I came to Honduras in March 1968 to teach at a Baptist church,

but when I found out I would be teaching only the kids of the wealthiest families, I wanted to look for a more authentic experience," she remembered. She heard about SAN and offered her services, in whatever capacity the organization needed, to the kids and housemothers in its brand-new Miraflores compound.

"In addition to caring for kids, Sor (Sister) María Rosa had figured out what was happening to women in Tegucigalpa," she said. "The best and brightest girls from the villages were coming to Tegus to better themselves, but they were being corrupted and falling on hard times, being seduced or impregnated or even prostituted. They were very vulnerable in the big city. So Sor talked to the village priests and asked them to send those young women directly to her, so they could work in her organization as housemothers and learn the skills to get a job."

Ryder met little Marco Antonio when his eyesight was already very impaired; he was going blind. She and Sister María Rosa estimated the child to be 18 months old, but in retrospect, given his unexpectedly early puberty, Ryder concluded he might have been as old as three years.

"I heard that his mother had gone blind during pregnancy," she said. "They lived in a typical home where the door opened up right on the curb, so when he started crawling, she had to tie a rope to his wrist or ankle to keep him from going into the street. When I met him his mother had already died and he was walking a little. He could see a little, but would look out only from under his eyelashes."

Ryder tried to take him to several ophthalmologists in Tegucigalpa. She said the doctors laughed at her because they knew neither she nor Sister María Rosa had any money to pay them. So she asked permission to take Marco Antonio, nicknamed Tony, home to Michigan to get him the care he needed.

"It was a bit of a splash when I got home and hadn't told my mother I was bringing a child with me!" she laughed.

Ryder and her mother, who worked at University of Michigan Hospitals, found doctors willing to donate their time to help. Tony's diagnosis was congenital nystagmus, an involuntary movement of the eye muscles that don't allow the eyes to focus. No surgical correction was available, but the doctors would strengthen his eyes with progressively stronger lenses.

Sister María Rosa came to Ann Arbor at least three times to visit and help raise funds for Tony's continued care. She and Ryder agreed that, because his mother had died, it would be best for Tony to stay in Michigan, where he could get better care. He was adopted and raised near Detroit by a family with whom Ryder has kept in touch. Today Tony lives in Boulder, Colorado, and has completed a college degree in criminal justice. He is legally blind, but Ryder reported that he can "sort of" see enough to get around.

Ryder said her experience with Sister María Rosa had a profound effect on the rest of her life and especially her career choice. When she finished college, Tony's adoptive father helped Ryder find a job in the Michigan state health department: Ryder worked with migrant families to find day care for their children. From there she got involved in social work programs to help migrants in Michigan and eventually Texas, where the National Center for Farmworker Health today strives to improve the health of migrant workers and their families.

"Most of the migrant families I worked with came from Mexico, but many were originally immigrants from Honduras, Guatemala, and Nicaragua," she noted. "It's serendipity that Sor had such a strong influence on me and inspired my work so many years into the future. I don't think it's a coincidence when people's lives brush up against each other this way."

Ryder returned to Honduras with Tony to visit SAN several years before Sister María Rosa's death.

"When I told her I was thinking of coming, she said, 'Come fast,

I'm old,'" laughed Ryder. "When I got there I was tickled to see she still lives in the same buildings in Miraflores."

It was important for Tony to visit Honduras, Ryder said, and to understand that he was better off being adopted into a U.S. family.

"I asked Sor in private whether it was right to take him to the U.S. as a baby," she said. "She told me that with his visual and developmental problems, he wouldn't have survived in Honduras."

Ryder said she learned from Sister María Rosa that aiding one person or family at a time can have a domino or ripple effect that carries on to the next generation. Ryder chose for herself a career very close to Sister María Rosa's: providing help and health care to the poorest of the poor, which in the United States is the immigrant population.

"Sor had an ability to galvanize people to do the right thing," Ryder said. "The fact she could do what she did in such an impoverished country is absolutely miraculous. I think it has to do with specific people and how prepared they are at that moment to receive what she has to offer, to go beyond being self-centered. If we are open to what she shares, she has a profound influence on our lives."

CHAPTER 4

PERMISSION GRANTED

SISTER MARÍA ROSA WINS APPROVAL—
BUT NO FUNDING—TO CREATE
SOCIEDAD AMIGOS DE LOS NIÑOS

--"There's always room for one more."--

By 1966 powerful visions of children's homes were invading Sister María Rosa's dreams: She was seeing little chimneys on rooftops with smoke coming out of each imaginary house.

"I was thinking, 'How long will I wait for two Sisters willing to come with me while kids are waiting in prison and sleeping on the streets?'" Sister María Rosa remembered.

She decided it was time to ask permission of her religious order to make those homes—with or without the company of other members of her religious community. The nuns at La Policlínica told her she would have to travel to the Milwaukee motherhouse to ask. The prospect was daunting: In 15 years she had still not found any other Sister in Honduras who was able or willing to join her in the immense responsibility of raising abandoned and abused children, children with real problems and dire needs.

"This is not like teaching school or working in a hospital," she said. "You have to have a special vocation, given by God, to work with children. There are no days off. Just because you are a religious doesn't mean you have the patience to work with children and their problems. You can't say to a child, 'Don't play now; it's time for prayer.' What the child needs at that moment—that's your prayer."

Some of Sister María Rosa's friends bought her a ticket to Milwaukee, where she asked her Mother Superior to make an exception to the rules and let her begin her project on her own. She reported that she would never find another Sister to come work with her, to leave La Policlínica or any other Tegucigalpa hospital or school.

"I told her, 'Can you blame me just because I can't find another crazy woman who feels this same vocation?'" Sister María Rosa said. "I knew that God wanted this and my duty was to do what God wanted me to do. He was pointing my whole life toward this work and making my whole life ready for this work. I was always going to do this. So I had to ask permission to break the rules, because this was not the way my community worked at that time.

"I think rules have to be broken when they don't work, don't you?" she asked playfully.

She reiterated that this project was not simply an idea; it was her vocation. "How could the community hold me back if God wanted me to do it?" she protested. "It wasn't an easy thing, but I had such faith in it. I told all the Sisters, 'You asked me why I wanted to be a Sister, and I told you it was because I want to work for the orphans and poor children of

Honduras. You accepted me that way, so can you give me permission to do that work now?'"

She presented her case to the Mother Superior and waited several days for an answer. One afternoon while Sister María Rosa was walking the Stations of the Cross in the garden, she was summoned to the office. On the way she prayed, "Lord, if the answer is no, please help me erase this plan from my mind." Her Mother Superior surprised her with a yes. Then she gave Sister María Rosa the conditions: The School Sisters approved her mission but could not support her with money or staffing. These children's homes would be purely Sister María Rosa's project, not the community's—which sounded like a negative outcome but was actually fortuitous for someone already used to doing things her own way.

"It wasn't easy for me to hear, because as a member of the order I thought I would get help if I asked for it," Sister María Rosa remembered. "But I quickly realized it was OK, and the Lord must want it that way. I said to myself, 'María Rosa, don't worry. If the Sisters don't send you, you are not under holy obedience in this work.'" She could make her own decisions without asking permission of anyone. She also knew that having a Honduran staff rather than nuns from Germany or America would show the people of Honduras that it is their duty to take care of poor children in their own country—a conviction central to her organization's long-term sustainability.

Sister María Rosa returned to Honduras, where in March 1966, at age 39, she founded Sociedad Amigos de los Niños. Members of Reyes Irene Valenzuela's local church retreat group helped legally form the organization for her.

"A man named Roberto Zacapa had written the paperwork, and then they invited me and others to join the society," said Doña Regina Aguilar de Paz, the wife of a former Honduran ambassador to Germany who served as SAN's board secretary from 1966 to 2013. She was well known in Tegucigalpa for her philanthropy then as now; she is typical of the influential people Sister María Rosa attracted to her organization from the start. "We knew Sister María Rosa was willing to do the work," she continued. "She just had to get the permission from the nuns."

Sister María Rosa still worked nights at the hospital but went out in the afternoons with Reyes to pursue a location for SAN's first children's homes—the ten houses she commissioned in the brand-new Miraflores neighborhood but didn't realize she had to pay for. When the houses were completed, the builder called Sister María Rosa's convent and left a message that she had 15 days to make the $5,000 down payment—an impossible sum. "I knew my religious order would not help pay for that because this was my work, not theirs," she said. "I had to trust that if the Lord wanted me to do this, He would help me somehow."

That same week at La Policlínica, Sister María Rosa cared for the wife of an American diplomat. The woman spoke no Spanish, and Sister María Rosa offered herself, with what she called her "poor little English," as a translator. She stayed with the American for several days and nights. When the woman was discharged, she asked her husband to give this nice little nun a gift for her care and companionship. The diplomat asked Sister María Rosa if there was anything that she needed.

"I told him that I didn't need anything for myself, since I am a religious and the community gives me everything," Sister María Rosa said. "Then I remembered my down payment on the houses!" She told him all about SAN and her homes for poor children. He replied that he was sorry—he didn't have that much money—but then he told her about a meeting the next morning at the American Embassy where she might present her needs.

"So I went with my businesswoman friend and board member Reyes," she recounted. "We brought another board member and the bylaws—thank God we had already made them!—to get the American Embassy to believe in our work. We didn't know it at first, but the meeting was about the blessed President Kennedy's Alliance for Progress grant program [from the U.S. Agency for International Development]. I told them about the children living on the streets and in the prisons, which they knew about but didn't think anyone was crazy enough to take those children in. I told them I had ordered ten homes but I didn't know I had to pay for them, and they were all laughing at the silly nun who thinks everything will just be given to her! But then they said, 'Yes, we want to help you.'" After that day, Sister María Rosa always added the honorific "blessed" in front of President John F. Kennedy's name every time she said it.

The grant covered the down payment but stipulated that Sister María Rosa had to finance the mortgages for every house. So she set out on a scavenger hunt to collect signatures from the only people she knew could pay: her board of directors, including the richest man in Honduras as he sat on a plane waiting to take off.

The timing of Sister María Rosa's vision of safe, loving homes for neglected children was urgent: In the 1960s unemployment was rampant in Honduras as rural workers displaced by industrial agriculture flocked to the cities and competed for already scarce jobs. The per capita income was around $150 per year, with two-thirds of families earning less than $40 a month. Fifty-five percent of the population was illiterate. Thousands of children were abandoned—many by single mothers who had themselves been abandoned by their children's fathers. More than half the population was under 15, and only a third of registered births listed a father.

SAN was created against a backdrop of social and economic desperation, but this was Sister María Rosa's venue, her time, and her plan. She knew exactly where she would get her first charges: the overcrowded Central Penitentiary in Tegucigalpa, where by custom children up to age 12 lived in a filthy cell with an incarcerated parent. In many cases, a mother with an incarcerated husband would turn her children over to their father in jail, saying she could not support them and at least in prison they would have shelter and food. There were also mothers in prison who chose to keep their children inside with them versus with their fathers or other relatives.

"It was terrible, because the men and the women were housed together in the prison," Sister María Rosa elaborated. "The mothers tried to protect their children so no men would touch them, but so many of those children were already harmed. I had to get them out of there right away."

One day, she marched boldly into the prison and brought out 14 young children for a field trip to see her new empty houses where they might eventually live. Some who were born in prison had never even been outside the walls. Once the kids were outside, however, the prison director informed Sister María Rosa that she could not bring them back. The mothers inside wanted her to keep them.

And so, after years of dreaming about sheltering, feeding, and loving children in need, Sister María Rosa suddenly had

14 to care for: hungry, dirty, abused, and antisocial from a life bereft of toys, school, good nutrition, and mental stimulation. Ready or not, SAN had its first family.

"I had just wanted to show them the homes, so they would tell others not to be afraid to come," she said. "All I had were sandwiches I had bought for their visit. The houses were empty, with no beds, no food, nothing. And here were the children."

She went to La Policlínica and gave notice that she wouldn't be returning to her nursing job, now that she was a mother of 14. Then she set priorities: beds, food, clothing. The U.S. Embassy donated military cots, but no bedding. Sister María Rosa tried to buy sheets on credit, but the storekeeper denied her, so she went to the School Sisters in Tegucigalpa, who gathered enough bedding for 14 beds. A policeman serving as a watchman for the homes helped cut and sew bolts of cloth into blankets. SAN's board of directors bought food and staples. For the rest of the children's needs, Sister María Rosa went back to her friend Reyes's church retreat group, an influential collection of people that included the American ambassador, Joseph John Jova.

"I asked permission to speak to those people and said, 'You might be feeling bad because you think you haven't done enough to help the poor. But now you can have a project!'" she smiled with excitement. "I took them with me and they cried to see the children. The kids didn't look so nice. Some of them had never had a shower. It took weeks to get those kids clean of the smell of the prison."

Within a day or two, members of Reyes's group sent a stove, refrigerator, table and chairs, milk, bread, and other food. These women and other friends from La Policlínica came every night for weeks to help feed and bathe the children, play with them, dress them in their first clean clothes, and comfort them in the absence of their mothers. The kids needed to know they were in a safe, stable place, known and cared for by loving adults. Sister María Rosa knew this intimately from her own childhood as an orphan and knew how to provide it.

"Life, love, patience—and big arms. We have to give them that," Sister María Rosa declared. "To me, the only way to solve poverty or misery is by giving children good health, good training, and good education. We have to recognize that these children are the image of God, and then love them and respect them and be even more than a mother and father to them. Every child had a little emptiness inside that we had to fill in order that they could grow and be someone different one day. My place in this world is to take care of each child, one by one. What happens after that is the Lord's."

The rest of SAN's houses filled quickly as news of Sister María Rosa's homes for neglected children swept through the country, especially in the capital.

"I cleaned the bridges of children begging and took the children abandoned by their mothers at the hospitals," Sister María Rosa reported. "The street kids were sleeping in the atrium of the church, sleeping in parks on top of cardboard. I could see them from the fourth-floor window of the hospital. These were abandoned children. I didn't ask them why they were in the streets; I just took them in."

She also went back to the prison to bring out more children living inside.

"After her first kids came from the prison, Sor María Rosa was horrified that babies and even teenage girls were still living in the prisons with no separation from the men," said Doctor Norman Powell, who worked with SAN as a Peace Corps volunteer in 1968 and '69. "It was awful: During the day the kids would go out of the prison, beg on the streets, and come back with food and money for the parents. So Sor convinced the wife of the president, who was in charge of all social service programs for kids, to let her go into prison again and take the kids out. It was very dramatic: One time she got the army to go in with their trucks and she brought more than a hundred kids out to her houses."

In addition, she gave shelter to those who walked alone from rural villages for hours or days to find "the nun who helps children." One abandoned 12-year-old boy tugged on Sister María Rosa's habit outside the supermarket and said, "I want to live with you and learn to work and make myself into a man," according to a 1968 *LIFE en Español* magazine photo essay by photographer David Mangurian.

By 1968, 145 children were living in the ten duplex homes in Miraflores, plus a nearby farm. SAN's board of directors was astonished at the rapid rate at which the houses filled with children. They had the financial means to support Sister María Rosa's project, but they worried about sustainability and soon told her she had reached capacity. Predictably, she ignored them, and told a story about the day she convinced them they were wrong.

"One day we were having a big board meeting, and they were telling me I had to stop taking more children," she said. "Then someone knocked on the door and I asked one of them to go see who was there. It was a lady who was pregnant, with a set of young twins in her arms, asking, 'Can you take care of my kids? I have to go to the hospital to have my baby!' The men got all excited, brought in the twins and wanted to call an ambulance for the mother. And I told them, 'If you can say no to this woman right here in front of you, then I will say no from now on about taking in more children.' So of course they stopped telling me to say no!"

Sister María Rosa leads children out of the Central Penitentiary to come live in her homes

PROFILE: THE PEACE CORPS MEMBER WHO WORKED WITH CHILDREN AT RISK

Doctor Norman W. Powell

Before Norman Powell came to Honduras with the Peace Corps in 1966, he had never been on an airplane or traveled outside of the United States. He was a sophomore at Howard University, unsure of what to do with his life, and impressed with President John F. Kennedy's idea of young people going abroad to help others. He could speak a little Spanish and had been a counselor for "children with emotional and behavioral disabilities" in college. So he was assigned to a Peace Corps program for juveniles with behavior problems at El Centro Juvenile de Jalteva, near the small rural town of Talanga, 30 miles north of Tegucigalpa. After 18 months, he was sent to Tegucigalpa, where he and his Peace Corps roommate founded a Boy Scout troop for young boys at risk.

"Sor María Rosa was just starting out with her projects, and we used one of her areas for a campout," Powell recalled. "She checked us out and got very excited about starting a Boy Scout program for SAN. Then she started really recruiting me heavily. She told me, 'Look, I'm just a little old nurse. I love kids but I've had no university training. You have training and experience with kids in the U.S. It would be great if you come help me organize the operation while I do the fundraising and political things.'

"She was incredibly charismatic, and I was smitten. She was a ball of fire, so energetic that most folks had a hard time keeping up with her. The Peace Corps was impressed by what Sor María Rosa was doing by herself, and they let me move from my previously assigned work site to work full-time with Sor."

Working as a director of admissions for the next year and a half, Powell said that he, Sister María Rosa, and everyone at SAN were activists in a troubled time in Latin America.

"We were activists for poor people, especially poor children," he said. "What she was doing was revolutionary. Her concept of placing groups of children in small family-like settings, as opposed to a huge institution with hundreds of kids, was innovative for those times. She was absolutely brilliant."

Powell witnessed the incredible changes in the lives of the abused and neglected children who came to live in her homes.

"I remember one time this woman came in with two kids around the ages of one and two," he said. "Their hair was full of lice and other things, they had bloated bellies from worms, they were each in a horrible condition. The mother told me, 'Please take them. I want them to be here with the nun.' Then she left and we never saw her again. The kids never saw her again. We put the two children into Sor's homes and a month later the lice were gone and the kids were running around with the other children, playing, looking beautiful and very happy."

Many times, Sister María Rosa came to Powell and said, "Get in the car, let's go! We have to go to pick up some kids!"

"Once we went to the public hospital into a back room where there was this feral child—emaciated, a head banger," he said. "I'd worked in residential treatment before and I recognized there was clearly a disability here. Sor said the girl had been left in the bed almost since she was a baby, hardly ever having been lifted up or hugged. Sor wanted to get her out of there, so we took her. At SAN, she screamed and yelled, had tantrums, and was a very difficult management challenge for the workers; she was extremely demanding. But over time you could see a huge change, just from her being fed and held and loved. When I came back to Honduras to visit in 1975, I saw this beautiful young girl coming home from school, looking very healthy. I could hardly recognize her.

"I thought to myself, in the U.S. we would have said she's emotionally disturbed and needs to be on medication or in a hospital. But in Honduras, Sor just moved her in with other kids, who were positive role models. To me that change felt like a miracle—a miracle of how caring and love can dramatically change someone."

Powell stayed in Honduras for three years, one extra year beyond his Peace Corps obligation. Back home he transferred to The American University in Washington, DC, and earned his degree in Latin American Area Studies and Spanish from the School of International Service. At The American University, he also earned a master's degree and later a doctorate in special education (in emotional and behavioral disorders) with minors in administration and family systems. During his entire professional life, he has continued to work on the local, national, and international level with children and youth at risk. He has directed numerous programs for children and youth at risk and served on the faculty of several universities around the country. After 22 years at Eastern Kentucky University as an associate professor in Educational Leadership and Policy Studies, he was made professor emeritus by the Board of Regents in the spring of 2020.

Powell said his year and a half with Sister María Rosa and his time in the Peace Corps led him directly to his lifelong passion and professional career. He believes he gained a lot of confidence in his field after being trusted with so much responsibility in Honduras.

"I ended up doing many things down there that I never would have been able to do in the U.S.," he said. "I was very quiet in high school and college, always terrified when I had to speak in front of a group. But I saw Sor get up in front of hundreds of people and make it seem like no big deal."

He considers Sister María Rosa "one of the smartest people that I've ever known."

"Here we were in one of the least developed countries in the world, with such a lack of education and literacy and opportunity," he said. "It was amazing to see things happen that were so positive for people. Sor created a lot of that. My time with her changed my life in so many ways, I was already interested in working with children before I went to Honduras, but my experience with Sor María Rosa really increased my passion for that work. And it gave me tremendous insight into Latin America, about poverty and politics, about people, and I've used that in everything I've done ever since. My experience in Honduras with Sor María Rosa had a profound and positive impact on my life."

CHAPTER 5

BURSTING AT THE SEAMS

SISTER MARÍA ROSA'S HOMES OVERFLOW WITH CHILDREN AS SAN OVERFLOWS INTO CENTRAL AND SOUTH AMERICA

--*"To save these children living on the city streets, you have to have strength and too much love to give each child all the care he has been missing since birth. You almost need to put them back into the womb to be born again, to help grow that dignity inside them."*--

Within a year or two of its founding, SAN's homes were brimming over with kids. Sister María Rosa's project needed an expansion—a second village of children's homes that could take in about 80 orphans from the public hospital and another 50 children growing up in prison.

SAN's original board of directors included very influential and wealthy men and women: Regina Aguilar de Paz, Nicolás Atala, Pedro Atala, José Rafael Ferrari, Oscar Kafati, Salomón Kafati, Eduardo Kawas, Manuel Villeda Toledo, and Reyes Valenzuela, among others. Several of them owned or managed television and radio stations. They approached

Sister María Rosa in December 1967 with what was then a novel request: Would she lead a 12-hour telethon to raise funds for SAN to build a "Children's City"? Once she agreed, they asked the nun to pray that the light bulbs in their equipment would last that long—they had never attempted such lengthy programming! By the end of the telethon she had gathered more than $70,000 in money and donated goods from both Hondurans and foreigners.

Sister María Rosa achieved the unlikely with that telethon and another she led the next year: She instigated the generosity of others in a poor and troubled country. The president and the richest families contributed. Foreigners contributed. Even the poor donated to the poor. Children went door to door in Tegucigalpa collecting money. In his 1968 *LIFE en Español* magazine essay about SAN, David Mangurian wrote of a 13-year-old boy who arrived at the TV studio to donate what he had earned selling gum on the street: the equivalent of 25 cents.

The telethon windfalls were vital to SAN's goal of funding itself rather than relying solely on the pockets of its board of directors. On April 14, 1970, Sister María Rosa inaugurated the second children's village in Tegucigalpa's Colonia Kennedy neighborhood. SAN built ten blocks of four homes each, all surrounding a central playground. In each home, just as in Colonia Miraflores, eight children lived with a "mother" or "auntie" who cooked for them, dressed and bathed them, and supervised their outings, school attendance, homework and chores. The village founded a school for kindergarten through second grade; this gave the younger children a strong basic formation before integrating them into the public schools by grade three. Most of these children had had no schooling at all before living in SAN homes, so kids of all ages populated the kindergarten.

SAN's work soon attracted attention from afar. In Central Europe, the S.O.S. Kinderdorf organization had been creating small-group homes for orphans for more than 20 years. Its founder, Austrian Hermann Gmeiner, had lost his mother as a very young child, just like Sister María Rosa had. After witnessing the suffering of war orphans during World War II, he gave up medical school to establish the first S.O.S. children's village in 1949 near the Tyrolean town of Imst in western Austria. Over the next two decades he founded villages in Italy, France, and Germany. His work continues today in more than 550 S.O.S. Children's Villages and 700 S.O.S. Youth programs in 136 countries.

From his own childhood experiences, Gmeiner shared Sister María Rosa's conviction that children must be raised in a home of their own rather than an impersonal orphanage. Like her, he believed that children without parents suffer greatly without personal, individual attention, and that love and care within a "normal" home would teach children how to take their place in society and be responsible for their own families as adults. Gmeiner's homes were very similar to Sister María Rosa's homes. Each had a substitute mother who cared for orphaned children who resided together as brothers and sisters, sharing meals and chores, attending school together—living as a family.

In 1968, Gmeiner invited Sister María Rosa to Germany, where SAN and S.O.S. Kinderdorf joined forces. Their partnership, called SAN Aldeas S.O.S., resulted in Sister María Rosa's oversight of hundreds of children's homes throughout Central America—500 in Honduras alone—over the next two decades.

Around this time Sister María Rosa also attracted a partner in her work, but not from her own community of Sisters. Father Willie Arsenault, known in Honduras as Padre Guillermo, was a missionary priest from Quebec's Gaspé Peninsula serving in Tegucigalpa. He came to Sister María Rosa's Miraflores compound to meet the "crazy little nun" about whom he'd heard rumors. He witnessed what she was accomplishing with poor children, and he stayed. He told Sister María Rosa that this work on the front lines of poverty was exactly what he came to Honduras to do. He helped build the first church at Colonia Kennedy and another in Miraflores, and was deputy director of SAN for its first 20 years.

They made a tremendous team: Father Willie was a planner and organizer and Sister María Rosa had the vision and sensitive maternal instincts.

"Father Willie would say that he was the brain of SAN and I was the crazy heart," said Sister María Rosa. "Well, to work for God is a little crazy, I guess. In the meetings I would go on and on about a new idea and everyone would look confused. So he would tell them, 'Just listen to her for now. Afterward, I'll tell you exactly what you need to do.' He was a simple man, very well trained, a good organizer. His family was really big—14 or 16 kids. Everybody loved Father Willie, and he was like a father image to my kids."

"Father Willie was the guy who made it all work," noted Doctor Jim McCallum, a Canadian oral surgeon who started visiting SAN in 1979. "Sister María Rosa was the one with the big ideas and dreams, but Father Willie was always there working in the background, never in the limelight."

"Padre Guillermo was probably the only person she would listen to," noted Powell, the Peace Corps volunteer.

"Sometimes they would fuss and argue and she would say, 'You're the only one who can make me do things I don't want to do!' He was the only one who could handle her."

৩৯৫৯

BY 1973 ANOTHER CHILDREN'S VILLAGE WAS COMPLETED AT Choloma, near San Pedro Sula, the second largest city in Honduras. This village of 32 homes had outdoor play areas, a kindergarten, sewing classes for the housemothers, and an agricultural area where some of the older boys harvested vegetables and raised cows, pigs, and rabbits. Sister María Rosa founded additional children's homes in La Ceiba, Tela, and Valle de Angeles, the last one for children with all types of disabilities.

The reputation of SAN Aldeas S.O.S. spilled over into neighboring countries. Throughout the 1970s Sister María Rosa was called all over Central America to share her expertise and start new homes for children, often after those countries suffered earthquakes or hurricanes with great loss of life and breakups of families. She became an expert in disaster recovery and rebuilding the lives of children. In 1972 Rosario Murillo, the First Lady of Nicaragua, summoned her for help after a devastating earthquake. In 1976 Sister María Rosa founded new children's villages in Ecuador and in Guatemala in the cities of San Juan Sacatepéquez and Quetzaltenango. In 1978 she rescued 156 children from her SAN Aldeas S.O.S. village in Estelí, Nicaragua, a war zone of strife against the Somoza government, and moved them over the border into Honduras.

She traveled frequently to Europe to promote the SAN Aldeas S.O.S. projects. As a nun with a fifth-grade education, traveling and public speaking did not come easily to Sister María Rosa. "It was difficult for me to travel when there was so much going on here at home," she said. "But I went because they needed me and I worked very hard to get sponsors for my children. S.O.S. thought that since I was from the Third World I could speak better about the needs than they could."

From those European fundraising trips Sister María Rosa developed her own rule of thumb for speeches: She never wrote out ahead of time what she would say to an audience. This might sound illogical or even irresponsible, but she had immense trust that the words that needed to be spoken would come to her. "When I speak in public I stand up, say hello, and then the words just follow," she explained. "I don't know what I am going to say; I don't have the training or the schooling. I just pray, 'Lord, I can't make this speech myself, but You know what these people need to hear.' And then He puts the words there, like rain in my mind. If you ask me in the next hour what I just said, I usually don't know.

"Sometimes in Europe they would ask me ahead of time what I was going to say so the translators could have it ready for a lot of people speaking a lot of different languages. I could never tell them because if I say it ahead of time, then they are my words, not God's. Since He is a spirit, He uses my body and my tongue. But He also needs some space!"

Overseeing SAN Aldeas S.O.S. throughout Central and South America was a huge undertaking, rewarding work that could have kept Sister María Rosa busy for the rest of her life. Local sponsorships helped support the Honduran children—some Honduran families sponsored ten kids apiece. And a Canadian NGO called Help Honduras Foundation, founded by Father Tim Coughlan and Christine and David

Stewart, helped attract child sponsors abroad. Still, the critical needs of the poor on the streets of Tegucigalpa rose right in front of her face all the time. So Sister María Rosa responded, whether or not it went along with the original vision of SAN Aldeas S.O.S. to save, house, and educate orphans only.

For example, she believed that teenagers, with or without parents, face special challenges in their adolescent development and need to continue their education and learn trades to make a living. By S.O.S. policy, however, teens had to leave the S.O.S. villages at the cut-off age of 13. So she created a Youth House in Miraflores for 80 adolescent boys from the villages, offering workshops in agriculture, carpentry, bricklaying, plumbing, tailoring, shoemaking, and mechanics. The boys still in elementary school studied early in the day and squeezed in ten weekly hours of vocational training. The older teen boys worked five hours a day and studied the rest of the time. Anyone over age 15 paid for school, books, clothing, and general expenses of the house with part of his earnings. By age 18 the boys were encouraged to earn their own living.

For young women, Sister María Rosa started the Youth Home of San Martín de Porres, which offered elementary and high school classes, along with instruction in sewing, cooking, and crafts. The older girls, like the boys, worked to pay for their studies and clothing. Next she founded a home called Mary Immaculate in the southern Honduras town of Choluteca. This house was a temporary stop for older girls who were far behind their chronological age in school. Here they could study without the humiliation of being so much older than the other students and without the extra pressure to catch up quickly. Younger children with particularly challenging physical problems or psychological needs came here as well; they received individualized therapy to see if they might eventually be able to join the SAN Aldeas S.O.S. village in Colonia Kennedy.

Sister María Rosa was also troubled by the growing problem of street women, unwed mothers, and abandoned wives giving birth to numerous children, many of whom would end up in her villages after living on the streets of Tegucigalpa for years. Sister María Rosa wanted these women, condemned by their families and Honduran society, to change their ways and learn their duties as mothers. In February 1971 she began an experimental project she called Rehabilitation of Unwed Mothers With Their Children. Hogar La Esperanza (Hope House) in Comayagua was dedicated to the physical, economic, spiritual, and moral care of destitute women and their kids. Unwed mothers lived here for two years at a time, worked in home industries to learn a marketable trade, and raised their children in a secure environment with an onsite daycare school. Sister María Rosa's own sister, Paula, came with her children to help with the project and its startup businesses in tortilla- and tamale-making and dressmaking. By 1975, 28 mothers and 81 children were part of this program.

With a special love and talent for agriculture, Sister María Rosa started several farms or farming co-ops around this time, too. In 1975 in Zamoranito, a rural area outside Tegucigalpa, Sister María Rosa founded an agricultural youth farm for teenage boys, with help again from Christine Stewart of Canada. Young men lived in 20 houses on the property, farmed rice, corn, and beans, and cared for cattle, pigs, chickens, and bees. The boys also attended workshops in carpentry, welding, electric work, auto mechanics, plumbing, shoemaking and tailoring, and other trades. Up to 500 young adults at a time lived there or came for education; many SAN employees today remember training in multiple trades at Zamoranito when they were young. "Every man or woman needs to learn how to do two or three things, in case one doesn't work out," Sister María Rosa explained. "Then they will be self-sufficient."

In 1977 Sister María Rosa started a small financial cooperative to help young Hondurans, especially her own children, secure startup loans for small businesses. Co-op Padre Guillermo Arsenault, named after Father Willie, is still in business today. With the help of a group of under-employed Honduran physicians, Sister María Rosa also organized La Asociación Apostoles de la Salud (Apostles of Health) to deliver medicine donated by the Canadian government to villages and hamlets. This project established up to 100 rural clinics in remote rural areas of Honduras.

Except for the banking co-op, none of these projects continues today, although other urgent programs have taken their places. Many of the older projects ran their course, serving an acute need at a certain time. These homes, farms, and enterprises were so countercultural for the 1960s and '70s, it's a wonder they worked at all. Few if any agencies or NGOs in Honduras focused attention on poor children and families at that time, but these initiatives were in lockstep with Sister María Rosa's goal to raise the dignity of women, children, and families. There was no particular rhyme or reason, no institutional philosophy to her actions; she simply responded with concern for the women and children in front of her, regardless of what the government or social agencies were doing. She made projects for the young, the old, the hungry, the rural poor, the uneducated, and the sick.

"People thought Sister was crazy for starting all these projects, but I thought she was a saint for doing it," said Francisco "Pancho" Paz, SAN's development director. Paz was raised at SAN by his mother, who worked with Sister María Rosa as a nurse at La Policlínica. "Sister just saw these needs and she responded with faith. She helped me a lot in life. I was blessed to know Sister since the day I was born— she was in the delivery room because she worked with my mother. When I was old enough, she got me a scholarship to go study agriculture in the United States. After I finished that, she gave me a job on her farm in Zamoranito, managing some of the trade shops, before I eventually went back to the U.S. to get my bachelor's degree.

"In Honduras sometimes it seems like nobody has the impulse to think of projects that will actually help people," Paz continued. "Not Sister. She just started something wherever she saw people having difficulty. Once when I was in high school she sent me and some other boys to a co-op near Tela to work with some old farmers who needed help. Her idea was that the boys would provide new blood for the old men, and the old men could share land and experience with the boys. Her ideas were very, very good. They worked for so many people and so many projects."

So most of SAN's early life-saving programs sprang full-blown out of Sister María Rosa's own volition and courage rather than any measured, detailed planning. Again and again she launched difficult projects with significant risks to beneficiaries and her own organization. Did the possibility of failure cross her mind? Were the endless acute needs of poor women and children the slightest bit daunting to her? She downplayed her daring and nerve, insisting that God put these projects specifically in front of her.

"My madness is to love and serve the poorest people—who are the wealth of God. When somebody knocks, I open, and that's it," Sister María Rosa said. "Here, if you are not a little crazy, you can't do anything. The crazy are not afraid."

Sister María Rosa leads Honduras's first telethon in 1967

Sister María Rosa speaks to a crowd at the groundbreaking for her Kennedy neighborhood children's homes

PROFILE: THE CANADIAN ORAL SURGEON WHO STARTED AN NGO

Doctor Jim McCallum

Jim McCallum had no idea, when he met Sister María Rosa in 1980, that he and his family and friends would end up dedicating a huge chunk of their income, energy, and lives to SAN. An oral surgeon from Petersborough, Ontario, McCallum's first trip to Honduras happened by invitation of a friend who asked, "How would you like to go to Honduras and pull teeth?" The friend skipped out at the last minute, but McCallum went anyway and was so changed by the trip that he made immediate plans to go back. He had not even met Sister María Rosa yet.

"The needs in Honduras were so great," he told me. "I grew up poor. Anne, my wife, grew up poor. But this was a different level of poverty, and the experience of having a skill to offer really touched my heart. I wanted to go back and do more."

Back home in Ontario, McCallum joined the Help Honduras

Foundation (later renamed Horizons of Friendship), after founders Christine and David Stewart told him about the year they had spent working with Sister María Rosa's organization in the early 1970s. McCallum wanted to meet this nun. So on his second trip to Honduras in 1980 he and a friend split from their mission group for an afternoon and started asking Tegucigalpa taxi drivers if they knew where to find Sister María Rosa. With just her name, they made it to her office in the Miraflores neighborhood. She greeted them with "Let me show you around my new project," and walked them a block away to her brand-new San Roque Medical Clinic.

"She was so charismatic!" McCallum remembered. "She wasn't afraid to ask anyone for anything, and even though we just met her, she told us exactly what she wanted from us."

What she wanted was dental equipment. She took McCallum to an empty room and said, "I want you to send me everything I need for this room, my new dental clinic." She acted as if McCallum had appeared on her doorstep as an answer to her prayers at the precise moment she had been mulling over her children's dental care. Back home, he did exactly as she asked, sending dental equipment on the first of dozens of containers he would ship from Canada with anything Sister María Rosa needed: food, clothing, medicine, water filters, large equipment.

From that first meeting, their relationship evolved quickly.

"It just grew on itself," said McCallum. "I brought my family into it and it's been a big part of our lives for more than 40 years."

McCallum became Sister María Rosa's close advisor and another father figure to the children at SAN. Sister María Rosa could confide in McCallum in a way she couldn't with her own staff, since she was at the top of the organization. And he could offer critical suggestions to her that her own staff wouldn't dare bring up. He and Sister María Rosa were uniquely suited to become friends. Over coffee, he said, the two would "conspire to improve kids' lives."

"Some ideas worked, and some didn't," McCallum said. *"One idea was to plant a vineyard, so we got these strong vines and hired a guy to take care of it all. Then he was killed in a car accident and the grapes fell into ruin."*

Many more of their ideas were successful, though, and McCallum's collaboration resulted in some of SAN's most important projects, including the eventual conversion of Sister's rural Nuevo Paraíso property from a village for single mothers into a compound of children's homes.

In time McCallum resigned from the board of Horizons of Friendship, whose efforts had grown beyond Honduras to all of Central America. He incorporated his own not-for-profit, Friends of Honduran Children, in 1993, though he says the organization really started in the 1980s, when his family urged him to form his own group. His plans were loose: The organization would simply help SAN and Sister María Rosa in whatever ways were needed at any given moment. These loose plans grew into a million-dollar operation that today administers child sponsorships, facilitates mission trips to SAN and brigades into rural areas, and supports many building and renovation projects at Nuevo Paraíso and its clinic.

"The office was in our home basement; for decades our house was a supply depot for brigade groups and shipping containers going down to Honduras," he said. *"We never had any excess, but usually just enough to pay the bills. Sister would ask us for money where she wouldn't ask any others. One time she and I were dreaming over a cup of coffee about developing a carpentry woodworking shop for her kids. We talked about purchasing the equipment; we figured we needed $5,000. So I called home and said, 'Anne, what do we have in the bank right now?' And she told me, '$5,000.'"*

The lives of the three McCallum daughters were shaped, too, by their father's close partnership with Sister María Rosa. Anne

McCallum told a story of one of their first trips to Honduras and its effect on her girls.

"At one point a Honduran woman came up to us with her baby," *she recalled. "She had given birth to twins three or four months ago,* *but one had died, and this other one was really, really small, wrapped* *in a blanket. She walked over to our 12-year-old daughter and tried* *to give her the baby, urging her to take the child to Canada for a* *better chance at living. This act had an everlasting effect on our* *daughter, who told us, 'These people have so little; I will never ask* *for anything again'"*

Another of McCallum's daughters, diagnosed with multiple *myeloma after her third child was born, needed help at home. The* *McCallums arranged for a SAN teenager to come to Canada on a* *visa to be a nanny and to study English. She eventually continued* *her studies at a university in Ottawa.*

With her first request for dental equipment, Sister María Rosa *unknowingly gave McCallum the job to which he's dedicated much* *of his life. His Friends of Honduran Children organization, led* *currently by Anne Morawetz and Peter White, has sponsored* *hundreds of SAN kids and decades' worth of successful projects.*

"I look at my peers here in Canada, well off in their retirement," *McCallum said, "and sometimes I look back and see that maybe I* *might have done a few things differently. But the thing is, I never* *hesitated. It felt right. Our family never hesitated about going and* *helping in any way we could."*

He said he believes he and Sister María Rosa were good for each *other's faith.*

"Or at least she was good for mine," he grinned. "She called me *her spiritual boyfriend!"*

CHAPTER 6

DIVINE INTERRUPTIONS

SISTER MARÍA ROSA'S WORK IS BOLSTERED BY MYSTERIOUS SAVING GRACES

--"They are God's kids, not your kids or my kids.
You have to trust that He will take care of them."--

S ister María Rosa drew one important conclusion from the wild growth of SAN's programs in the 1970s and 1980s: Her plans matched God's Plan. She exercised both an intuitive knack for pinpointing the urgent needs of the poor and the chutzpah to try to fulfill those needs. These were gratifying days as Honduras and the world took note of SAN's first fruits: Previously destitute children were growing up in small-group family homes, attending school, learning trades, finding jobs, getting married, and educating their own children.

These two decades brought the first of dozens of official recognitions for Sister María Rosa's work. As early as 1969, three short years into her project, she was honored as a Distinguished Woman of Puerto Cortés, her hometown, which was the first award of its type in Central America. In 1970 she was awarded the Rotary Button and made an honorary member of the Rotary Club of Tegucigalpa. The Honduran government issued a postage stamp in her honor in 1971, recognizing her exceptional work on behalf of "handicapped children," among all the children she worked to save. In 1975 she received a gold medal from the women's affairs committee of the National Workers Federation of the North of Honduras and Hermann Gmeiner presented her a ceremonial ring when he named her S.O.S. Kinderdorf International's general coordinator for Central America and Ecuador.

In 1977 Sister María Rosa received the Good Samaritan Award from the National Catholic Development Conference in New York for "inspiring dedication to the needy with great humanitarian love." That same year, Honduran communities in New York and Chicago recognized her for her work "in favor of the homeless children of Honduras." In 1978 she was elected Mother of the Year by the Honduran Federation of Women's Associations. The next year, in a solemn town meeting held on the 400th anniversary of the founding of Tegucigalpa, she won an award called the Hoja de Liquidámbar—the Sweetgum Leaf, named for a majestic tree that grows in Tegucigalpa—for her humanitarian labor. Saint Francis Xavier University, in Antigonish, Nova Scotia, Canada, conferred on her an honorary doctorate in 1986, and in 1988 she won the Honduran Rotary Club's Extraordinary Woman award for services provided through SAN. She was named a Dame of the Americas by the National Council for Women's Rights in Mexico City in 1989, and Person of the Year by the Honduran government a year later.

Awards like these would keep pouring in over the next three decades.

Taking stock of her organization's success, Sister María Rosa attributed all of these accolades confidently to her Lord, declaring that God, not she, was doing the work and making these good things happen. People heard this over and over and grew curious: Just how and why *is* Sister María Rosa so successful in her ventures? Has she just been lucky over and over again, or does a higher being truly lend a hand in all she accomplishes? The word "saint" began to come up in context of her service to poor women and children. Her friends and coworkers offered the phrase "divine intervention" for all the times things went Sister María Rosa's way, often in unusual or unexpected fashion and not easily explained as chance. Some used the word "miracle" when her work was buoyed by mysterious saving graces that occurred at exactly the right moment.

Miracles get a bad rap at times, the concept cheapened by odd media outbursts over weeping Madonnas and grilled cheese Jesuses. Everyone assigns a different weight and meaning to the word, and some people are uncomfortable when unusual occurrences are called "divine intervention" without some kind of imprimatur or official church approval. The term "divine interruptions" might be more appropriate, since a miracle is often defined as a perceptible interruption in the laws of nature or probability.

In Sister María Rosa's life, those laws of probability were interrupted *a lot.*

Once in SAN's early years, Sister María Rosa found herself outside the penitentiary with 40 new children for her already-full homes. She hailed a city bus and asked the driver if he could help transport these kids to Miraflores even though she had no money to pay him. After he finished his route he came back with the bus for her and the children. When the bus reached her SAN compound, Sister María Rosa asked the driver to wait with the kids. She walked ahead alone to talk to her SAN staff, who were visibly upset. How could they possibly feed 40 more mouths or buy 40 more beds?

"I told them they could get mad at me later and say there is no room, but for now just welcome these new children," Sister María Rosa said.

The kids unloaded themselves from the bus. As it pulled away, a truck immediately arrived. with a surprise donation from a furniture store going out of business: exactly 40 beds.

"So my people said, 'Good! They have a place to sleep. But what will they eat?'" Sister Maria Rosa continued. Just then a second truck pulled up to deliver excess rations from the U.S. military that the Honduran officers had no place to store: eggs, bread, meats, and cheeses—unaffordable treasures to the poor in Honduras. A young man working at the airport had sent them to Sister María Rosa, who, he remembered, "had a lot of kids to feed."

"We ate off that truck for a month," Sister María Rosa smiled. "It was food we had never eaten before, food that we never ate again. We had to call friends to keep the food in their houses for us; we didn't even have room to store it all!"

Another time, Sister María Rosa was preparing to leave on a fundraising trip to Europe. Her staff begged her to leave some money with them to buy food and pay bills. She kept busy attending to other needs and they grew anxious as her flight time approached. Suddenly there was a knock on the door from a man who looked gaunt and tired. Sister María Rosa invited him in, made him tea, and sat down with him, all to the frustration of her staff, who realized she wouldn't have time to get money for them before her departure. The man told Sister María Rosa he lived in Guatemala and his mother had just died and left him an inheritance. He said he felt a strong urge to drive to Tegucigalpa, find the nun who helps children, and give this money to her *today*. He had driven all night without any police or military stopping him, even at the border. Before he left to return to Guatemala, he handed Sister María Rosa $48,000.

On her way out the door to the airport, Sister María Rosa tossed the money over to her staff, chiding them, "You people of little faith!"

Sister María Rosa played the lottery often and won at unusual times. In 1973, according to Francisco Picado, who worked with her for decades, one of SAN's workers, Nena Pedregal, was in danger of losing to a pawn shop the taxi she drove for income. When Sister María Rosa found out, she said, "Well, I don't have a way to help her, but I have a lottery ticket here." As the lottery numbers were announced, she asked everyone present to pray that if it was God's will, this ticket would win. Number by number the ticket won, and she immediately handed it over to Pedregal.

Longtime SAN staffers remember times when Sister María Rosa was successful in water-witching or dowsing, a pseudo-scientific method for finding water in dry land. During a water shortage in Tegucigalpa in the 1970s, she hired a drilling company and, under supervision of the local water authorities, used dowsing rods to try to locate water near her Colonia Kennedy compound. She asked all children and adults in her projects to pray to Saint Joseph, and on March 19, Saint Joseph's feast day, water cascaded out of the ground where she drilled.

Years later, she tried it again, searching her Nuevo Paraíso property for a water well so she could build her new village there. "A rich man who owned the adjacent property had dug all over to find water, but he never could," said Pancho Paz. "There were holes all over the place—big holes dug by a professional company. But Sister took two copper rods and walked around, holding them out. When they crossed, she told the company to dig there. And they hit water exactly where she told them. Twice. So now there are two wells at Nuevo." Her accuracy was very unusual and very fortunate, because it was expensive at the time to drill for water. Sister María Rosa would have had to pay the drilling company for every hole, even if it came up dry.

Sister María Rosa also had uncanny premonitions for natural disasters. She once turned around a group of her children on an overnight vacation in Guatemala on an uncomfortable hunch that something was wrong. "I took some children who were good in school with me to Guatemala," she remembered. "I was in the hotel at night and something told me to go back to Honduras. So I got the kids and we went home. Everyone was mad at me; the children wanted to see Guatemala. But we got home later that night, and when I woke up the next day the radio said that Guatemala had just had an earthquake. All the bridges were out; half of our hotel was gone."

The story of her most dramatic hunch became more and more uncomfortable for her to tell in her later years, until she didn't like to speak about it anymore. ("I feel it too strongly all over again," she told me.) On September 18, 1974, Sister María Rosa awoke with a sense of foreboding about a hurricane reported to have formed in the eastern Caribbean. Forecasters downplayed the storm; a civil aeronautics engineer at Toncontin Airport assured her the weather wasn't serious for Honduras. While many of her staff accused her of exaggeration, she packed up medicines, candles, first aid materials, and other supplies, and traveled from Tegucigalpa five hours north over the mountains to check on more than 125 children in her care in Choloma, near Puerto Cortés. She arrived to a deluge of rain as Hurricane Fifi skimmed Honduras's northern coast after reaching its peak intensity of 110 miles per hour.

The scene was dire. As writers Donald and Dorothy Stroetzel detailed in an article about Hurricane Fifi in the May 1977 issue of *The Rotarian* magazine, mudslides were pushing cars and buses off mountain passes, killing large numbers of people. Flash floods from two feet of rain were ripping apart homes and isolating entire villages. The concrete bridge spanning Choloma's Rio Blanco collapsed soon after Sister María Rosa's vehicle passed over, and a landslide of soil and boulders buried a hillside village just a few miles away.

In Choloma, the water was rising, and Sister María Rosa found that the housemothers had set the children on high rafters inside the houses because no one could swim. Shortly after 1 a.m., when the storm carried away a neighboring home, she ordered the adults to take the children outside to higher ground. Then she waded and swam through the homes—dodging floating furniture, doors swinging off their hinges, and swimming cows—to make sure everyone was out.

Sister María Rosa found no one, so she joined the kids and housemothers, who accounted for all the children. Then, above the shrill wind and pounding rain, Sister María Rosa heard something. It was very faint—a child's coo that she later described as "a cry in my heart." Then all was silent. No one else heard the sound. They pleaded with her to come to safety, but she plunged back into the flood. At one of the last houses she felt compelled to swim inside and found a small mattress about to float out the doorway. Off the side of the mattress dangled the hand of a two-year-old boy who was fast asleep. She carried the toddler out in her arms, wading and swimming through water up to her neck.

"I knew I heard *something*, so I just went; I didn't worry too much or think too much," Sister María Rosa said. "The Lord was there pushing me and thinking for me and doing for me. I listened to the voice because I was used to Him speaking to me all the time."

The housemothers and smaller children packed themselves into two cars, and SAN staff and older teens walked alongside them in the flooded road, pushing all their weight against the vehicles to keep them from floating away. Sister María Rosa walked barefoot; she had lost her shoes somewhere. They inched their way all night in the storm until they made it to a housing project on higher ground about two miles away, where families took them in and fed the children.

During the storm, a large mudslide blocked the Choloma River, creating a dam that held back a massive torrent of floodwater. On September 20, two days after the hurricane hit the Honduras coastline, a concrete bridge gave way upstream and the mudslide dam broke, resulting in an explosive flash flood which decimated Choloma and Sister María Rosa's houses. The children eventually returned to find their homes buried waist-deep in mud, their gardens destroyed, their chickens and cows and rabbits drowned.

A few fortuitous things happened, however. A maintenance man was able to dig up the freezer, filled with chicken and meat for a week's worth of meals; the food had stayed frozen without electricity in the cold mud. And although the bridges were washed out, Sister María Rosa's vehicle was able to make it down and up the banks of the Choloma River to go for supplies and a generator. When a policeman told her she would never get across without four-wheel drive, she yelled, "I am not a woman who waits!" and pressed on. Her truck was one of very few vehicles that could drive across the riverbed.

When the homes were cleaned out, the Choloma children's village became a hospital and refuge for hurricane victims, with Sister María Rosa coordinating relief efforts. For months, she listened to a ham radio and intercepted international aid shipments and visiting nurses and doctors, driving them from the San Pedro Sula airport straight to Choloma. She even signaled helicopters carrying medical supplies to land at her village by laying white curtains into a huge white cross as a landing pad.

It was widely reported that an estimated 2,800 to 5,000 people died in Choloma alone as Fifi walloped the north coast with floodwater, sand, mud, and afterward, disease. Choloma accounted for 20 to 25 percent of all fatalities across Central America for this hurricane. Because Sister María Rosa drove north that day on a premonition, however, not one hair on the heads of her children was harmed.

Certainly these extraordinary events in Sister María Rosa's history could be labeled lucky coincidences, without any hint of the supernatural. Her work could be deemed "miraculous" simply in that her programs were successful against all obstacles and odds at that chaotic time in that troubled country. Maybe it was simply her dauntless drive that resulted in wonderful outcomes, with no "divine interruptions" at all.

Still, listening to Sister María Rosa repeat over and over that God was executing a plan through her actions had an effect on people's minds and hearts. To many in Sister María Rosa's closest circle, miracles were absolutely possible in this woman's life because they witnessed on a daily basis her tête-à-têtes with God.

"She always got these messages from the Lord," said Doña Regina Aguilar de Paz, Sister María Rosa's longtime friend and SAN board member. "We just knew: Those were things that *had* to be done."

"Sister's closeness with God was amazing," said Mae Valenzuela, SAN's director of volunteer groups. "When we would have nothing to feed the children, she would simply say, 'Trust,' and then someone would come with a donation. This happened so many times. And she had such vision! How did she know the wells were there to make Nuevo Paraíso into the place it is today?"

"With Sister, there have just been so many events: medical miracles, logistical miracles, financial miracles, happenstance miracles," laughed Brian Smith, director of construction for the Cleveland Clinic who has been coming to volunteer with SAN since 2001. "I've been with new people who, after a medical event like the survival of a sick baby or someone with a trauma, will announce that they've just seen a miracle. I just laugh and tell them, 'Well, yeah. It happens here all the time!'"

Smith recounted one story when he took a mission group to Honduras and El Salvador. One college student became very ill and needed to get to the Cleveland Clinic's hospital in Florida as soon as possible. "It was 2 a.m. and I was on the phone with American Airlines trying to get two seats on the first flight out—for the young lady and for a nurse to go with her," he said. "The airline was telling me it would cost $2,800 extra and I was telling them, no, these people already have tickets, but they just need to change to this flight due to a health emergency. I was getting nowhere. Then Father Lorn Snow, one of our group members, walked into the room and said, 'I just talked to Sister and she's praying about this.' Lorn told me later that I was so frustrated I rolled my eyes at that. But the airline agent immediately came back on the phone and said, 'You're all set on the first flight out tomorrow morning. No charge.' This was after 90 minutes mostly on hold and within one minute of Lorn passing along the prayers."

⚜

I WITNESSED ANOTHER ONE OF THESE EXTRAORDINARY events myself. One morning on a 2010 mission trip, our team drove to SAN's Flor Azul residential farm school with an eight-foot-tall cross, constructed of two-by-fours and graffitied with the multicolored signatures of every SAN child and worker. We planned to add the names of the teenage boys who lived at Flor Azul to the cross during a blessing ceremony and then mount the cross on the hilltop overlooking the farm. That day rain was falling in vertical sheets, and clouds were wrapped like headscarves around the hilltop pine trees. We were not sure if Sister María Rosa, coming from Tegucigalpa with her driver, Sorto, could traverse the wet and rutted dirt road to make it to the cross raising, but her truck did eventually arrive. Sorto helped Sister María Rosa into the wheelchair she used sometimes because of painful lymphedema in her legs, and we all gathered in the yard. The rain conveniently slowed to a drizzle.

To keep the cross off the wet grass, two boys brought out some folding chairs from the dining hall and laid the wood gently across them. Father Chris Wadelton, a priest with our group, blessed the cross, telling the teenagers that their signatures would represent the Body of Christ on this cross without a corpus. When they huddled to sign it, however, the Sharpie markers wouldn't write on the wet wood. We quickly concluded that we needed to lug the cross indoors and dry it.

"Let me carry it! I want to carry it!"

The appeal came from the least able person there: Sister María Rosa. An octogenarian. In a wheelchair.

"I want to try," she insisted. "I want to feel a little of what our Lord felt walking to Calvary."

We were alarmed. How could Sister stand, much less walk, on her dusky red, swollen legs, while lifting this over-sized cross? It was very heavy; it took several men to heave it onto and off the roof of our bus as we transported it to SAN's projects for all the children to sign. There was no arguing with Sister María Rosa, however: She was going to carry this cross. (We learned later that she had been contemplating this feat ever since she signed the cross herself three days earlier in Tegucigalpa.)

Sister María Rosa slowly hoisted herself up from her wheelchair to stand. Four boys lifted the cross chest-high, parallel to the ground, and she shuffled over into the crook where the beams intersected. She tried to tip the cross onto her shoulder; she wanted to carry it alone. The boys were hesitant, though, shifting from one foot to the other, unwilling to lay the full weight on her. No words were spoken; the boys simply held on stubbornly to the foot, head, and one arm of the cross. So Sister María Rosa settled for the other arm; it was enough. Several teenagers lifted a red tarp high as a canopy over the cross and its carriers, and this procession crept slowly across the wet grass and rocks toward the Flor Azul dining hall. The boys matched the nun's labored pace.

She never stumbled, not even in the soft mud. When Sorto approached her with the wheelchair at the steps to the dining hall porch, she waved him off. With a dash of energy, she lifted her side of the cross up the uneven steps onto the porch and twice tilted the crossbeam vertically, to maneuver around corners and fit through the doorway. Finally, she and the boys deposited the cross on a long dining room table.

Sister María Rosa was exultant. "See? The Lord never gives us a cross too difficult to carry!" she proclaimed to the boys and all the visitors in attendance.

She did not stay for our procession up the hill to mount the cross. The rest of us took turns carrying the cross high over our heads in groups of six or eight, chattering about Sister María Rosa's unbreakable will and this unlikely feat of bearing such a load on her weak, ailing legs. Someone brought up the M-word: Was this some kind of miracle?

The next day, I asked Sister María Rosa how her legs were feeling. For many years, severe joint pain and muscle cramps had kept her awake at night, and I assumed she would be in great pain after walking under the cross. "I slept the whole night without waking once!" she told me with surprise. "This is the first night in months I haven't had terrible pain in my legs."

I figured that adrenaline had temporarily masked the pain and that her legs would feel the repercussions of that great exertion soon enough. So I asked her the next day: Still no leg pain? "It's really strange," she said. "I haven't slept so well and felt so good in a very long time."

Day Three: Still no leg pain, no night cramps. Was she somehow cured of her affliction?

No, as it turns out, but it was certainly a strange remission. Back home a month later I received an email from her. "My legs are back to their own ways, as painful as ever," she wrote. "So this is my own cross. But carrying it is never as painful as what our Lord had to endure."

Years later, I continue to wonder how she managed that heavy weight. Pure grit? Characteristic determination? A little divine interruption? I suppose what mattered most was that Sister María Rosa had achieved her aim. She had as usual gotten her way. She had carried her Lord's cross, if only for 60 feet, up some steps and across a porch. Maybe for a little while afterward, then, He carried hers.

So the stories of saving graces in Sister María Rosa's life are there for interpretation. When people asked her whether these episodes—and many, many others—constituted miracles in her life, she just waved it off as business as usual. Divine interruptions from God were not surprising or startling at all to Sister María Rosa. Rather, they rained down regularly in her life, like thunderstorms popping up from the heat of her good work.

The Honduran government issued a 1971
postage stamp in Sister María Rosa's honor

Sister María Rosa received an honorary
degree from Francis Xavier University in
Antigonish, Nova Scotia, Canada

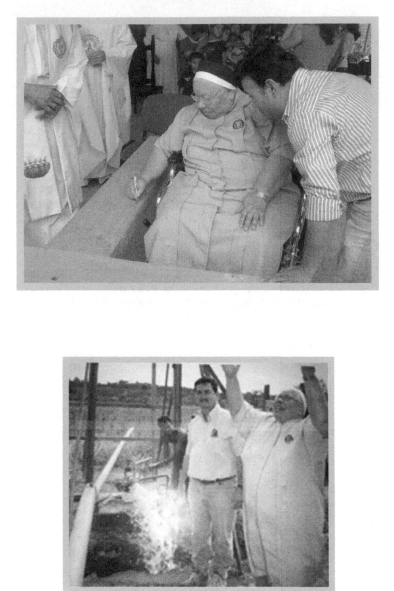

Sister María Rosa holds up her arms in prayer
after she finds water on her property

PROFILE: THE SHIPPING MAGNATE WHO BUILT A HOSPITAL

Daniel Meehan

Daniel Meehan laughed about the strange circumstances that called him to build a hospital for SAN and Sister María Rosa.

Meehan's career was in shipping. He had no background in health care or hospitals. As a young man, he graduated from New York's Maritime Academy and worked at sea until he got a Port of New York job with Ted Hansen Seaway Service. When the Saint Lawrence Seaway was opened to the Great Lakes, Meehan moved to Milwaukee to start the midwestern branch of Hansen's company. When Hansen retired, Meehan took over the whole company, running it from 1978 to 1996. At his own retirement he sold the company and started a philanthropic fund, the Meehan Family Foundation, to help, "in whatever way we are privileged, to give some degree of hope to God's special people," he said. His foundation supports religious missionary programs in 18 countries; through his charity he had encounters with Pope John Paul II, Mother Teresa, and three U.S. presidents.

Meehan met Sister María Rosa by chance in 1999 when he attended an event at the Milwaukee motherhouse of the School Sisters of Saint Francis. "There was no reason for me to be going over there," he recounted. "It was so out of character for me that the Holy Spirit had to have scheduled it. I had never even heard of the School Sisters of Saint Francis. But some girl from their development office called and invited me to the event. Why did I say yes?"

There he was introduced to Sister María Rosa, who was visiting Milwaukee for her jubilee reunion, and to Jim McCallum, from Peterborough, Ontario. McCallum and Sister María Rosa were discussing the need for a rural medical clinic at her children's village, Nuevo Paraíso.

"I was hooked by Sister María Rosa immediately," Meehan remembered. "I didn't know what she represented, what the School Sisters represented, but I fell in love with her and with all she was standing for. So I asked her if I could come visit her."

When he came to Honduras, Sister María Rosa gave him a tour of her projects.

"She had built these little houses at Nuevo Paraíso," he said. "There were about four people in each house—a mother and several kids. I did the math and figured she had a few hundred people there, mostly kids. So I asked her, 'What kind of health care do you have?' She said, 'Oh, Mr. Meehan, let me show you,' and she brought me to a tiny house with a waiting area outside under a small awning. Inside was just one room for a doctor who would come once a week. I could just imagine the lines of people waiting in the heat."

Meehan said he did something next that wasn't like him at all. He asked Sister María Rosa to bring an architect to her office the next day before Meehan was scheduled to fly home. He said he knew little about this sort of thing, but he and the architect were able to sketch a rough plan for a large clinic, with examination rooms and a large waiting room.

"The end result—the clinic we built—was not exactly that drawing, but the two of them understood that I was thinking of someplace big enough to serve all the people in the surrounding area as well," Meehan said. "The plans and drawings went back and forth from Honduras to Milwaukee for awhile, and then we were off and running."

The Santa Rosa de Lima Clinic, completed by the Meehan Foundation with help from local Rotarians and McCallum's Friends of Honduran Children organization, opened in 2000. Until his death in 2019, Meehan paid for updates and several additions. He believed his work with Sister María Rosa and the clinic, despite its ups and downs, its additions and closings, was preordained.

"It was all divine providence with her," he smiled. "The only time anything was a coincidence with Sister María Rosa is if God didn't want to take credit for it."

Meehan said he felt blessed by divine providence ever since he met Sister María Rosa. He told another story about Sister María Rosa inviting him to a special Mass in Honduras celebrating her 80th birthday. Meehan asked her what he could bring to honor this very special occasion.

"She replied instantly, 'an oil painting of my patron saint, Rosa de Lima,' and I told her she would have it," Meehan said.

He was unsuccessful, though, even after asking contacts at the Vatican for help.

"Driving to Chicago for one flight to Houston and another to Tegucigalpa, I was feeling pretty bad about myself," Meehan recalled. "But then, as we approached Tegus, there was a low ceiling of clouds that prevented us from landing there. They flew us to El Salvador instead. The pilot was getting ready to turn around and return us to

Houston, but they announced that any passenger could disembark at San Salvador if he signed off on liability, and I did that. To my relief, they even provided us with our baggage, and I arranged for a short flight to Tegus the next day.

"So I got into a taxi and headed into the city for the night. The driver asked which hotel I wished and I told him I didn't know of any and that he should choose. So we drove up to a hotel, I paid my fare, and walked in to find an art exhibit and sale in the lobby. I headed straight for two women sitting at the exhibit desk and asked, 'Do you have any paintings of Saint Rose of Lima for sale?' to which they replied, 'Yes, two oil paintings.'

"Mission accomplished! With the supreme help of Sister María Rosa's divine providence."

CHAPTER 7

STRUGGLES AND DOUBTS

SISTER MARÍA ROSA SOLDIERS ON THROUGH A MURDER, ECONOMIC COLLAPSE, AND THE BREAKUP OF A LONG PARTNERSHIP

--"I am trying to erase begging, trying to keep children from saying, 'I am poor; help me.' I tell my children, 'Your mother gave you birth. Now you are responsible for your life.' Once you are born, I say you have to get up and get going!"-

For Sister María Rosa, clarity about the Lord's will was never in short supply. Neither were challenges, impossible shortfalls of money and support, and tragedies that tested her faith and stamina.

The 1970s and 1980s sent the Honduran economy into a free fall. Coffee prices were in very steep decline on the international market and Honduras's other mainstay crop, bananas, was beleaguered by drought, disease, and natural disasters like Hurricane Fifi. Agricultural jobs were scarce (Honduras is nicknamed the Tibet of Central America for its mountainous, uncultivable terrain) and three-fourths of the population lived below the poverty line. Unemployment doubled from the late 1970s to 1983, so that more than half of the Honduran labor force was un- or underemployed by the start of the 1990s.

Because children and families are always the first casualties of poverty, SAN was busier than ever in its mission to house, protect, educate, heal, guide, and vocationally train young people toward self-sufficient lives. The violence and despair of the times, however, reached Sister María Rosa very personally in 1986, when Father Willie Arsenault, her friend and partner in SAN leadership, was murdered.

On March 21, 1986, two men arrived at SAN's farm at Zamoranito, calling for Father Willie by name. They asked him for money, but then shot the 54-year-old priest to death. The police called it a robbery, but people familiar with the case insist it was a political killing by Nicaraguan Contras camped throughout southern Honduras. A Canadian teacher who witnessed the shooting said that the men had the style of rifle carried by the Contras and the Honduran military, and wore "city shoes." The two men who were eventually caught and tried for the murder were Nicaraguan, identified by Honduran officials as Contra rebels fighting against the Nicaraguan government.

"Father Willie was very activist in helping poor folks," said Norman Powell, the Peace Corps volunteer. "He was quite controversial; he was involved in a co-op of farmers and worked at organizing the *campesinos*. He was also quite a good person."

People came from all over Honduras and the world to Father Willie's funeral, Sister María Rosa recalled.

"This country was upside down realizing that a priest could be killed here," she said. "But I think he always knew something was going to happen to him. His father showed me something when I traveled with his body to Canada. When Willie was away at university in Europe, he had sent a postcard home to his parents. It said, 'If something ever happens to me, don't worry. It's just the way God calls His people.' So, many years later when I called Canada at 3 a.m. to tell his father what had happened, his father carried that postcard to his mother. That's the way she found out Willie had died."

Father Willie's portrait hangs proudly in Sister María Rosa's office, and her banking co-op of 9,000 members carries his name. He was instrumental in making SAN's programs work effectively, and he was a beloved male influence for all of SAN's children. Perhaps his greatest contribution was his deep understanding and support of Sister María Rosa's methods, her motivation, and the great challenges she faced as a woman religious living and working mostly outside a religious community. Once when Father Willie noticed that Sister María Rosa was particularly overwhelmed with the hugeness of her project and the terrible poverty of her country, he went to a nearby seminary and "borrowed" three Canadian Sisters to stay awhile with her, to pray with her, to sing with her. A community of nuns in the area even asked her if she'd like to join their order. Sister María Rosa refused.

"Regardless of all the hard times, I would never step out from my community," she said. "The nuns came all the way from Germany to Honduras to bring me to their community, and that is where God wants me to be."

Certainly, Sister María Rosa was in frequent touch with the School Sisters of Saint Francis, both in Tegucigalpa and back in Milwaukee. Various Franciscan Sisters spent time at SAN from its earliest days, including Sisters Roswindis Kurz and Cristiane Emig. Emig stayed at SAN for three decades until she retired in 2015 and moved back to Germany; she founded a preschool and kindergarten for SAN kids so that their single mothers could work during the day. In 1974 Sister María Rosa was elected executive director of the Latin American Franciscan Union and coordinated the services and ministries of all the School Sisters of Saint Francis in Honduras, Costa Rica, Mexico, and Peru. Other School Sisters of Saint Francis assisted Sister María Rosa's projects by organizing child sponsorship from the United States and giving money to cover SAN salaries when the Honduran government payments fell short or were very late.

Sister María Rosa also founded a lay order of women, called Hermanas Contemplivas en Acción (Contemplative Sisters in Action), who lived in community and trained to work with children as housemothers and caregivers. Still, after Father Willie was killed, Sister María Rosa alone bore the daily responsibility for thousands of children. She lived a life very different from the other Tegucigalpa Sisters; she ran a busy, successful solo project financed by an influential and high-profile board of directors.

"María Rosa did have very unusual gifts for that time and place," noted her friend Sister Kathlyn Brenner. As executive director of the Chicago province of the School Sisters of Saint Francis from 1969 to 1975 and president of the community from 1992 to 2000, Brenner traveled extensively to visit and check on Sisters around the world, including her classmate María Rosa. "She always did reach out to the other Sisters in Tegucigalpa," Brenner continued. "But many of the Honduran women couldn't understand María Rosa. Not too many Sisters at the time would have encouraged such bold behavior or gone off with her to do what she was doing with those children."

Brenner confirmed that all Sister María Rosa got from her religious order when she left La Policlínica to start SAN was a verbal "Yes, we support you."

"We just didn't have the money to fund every Sister's dream," she said. "María Rosa got her financial support in other ways, from people in Honduras and later from North America. She got the project started, and then other Sisters did work with her in different ways over the years. Back in the United States, for example, we started a Friends of the Children office to manage donations and letters. But María Rosa kind of ran her own program. It was our mission to help simply because she was there."

Another challenge of the times was liberation theology, a religious movement that emphasized the perspective of the poor and pushed the Catholic church to take political and social action toward change. This meant the church often stood in direct opposition to Central America's military governments. In neighboring El Salvador on March 24, 1980, Archbishop Óscar Romero was assassinated by a far-right death squad, shot as he said Mass. Honduras was spared the civil wars fought in other Latin American countries, but the 1970s and 1980s were still marked by disappearances and violence. Brenner's own cousin, activist Jesuit Father James Carney, disappeared and was allegedly killed in Honduras in 1983 after many years of serving insurgents there. Brenner said she always wanted to go take his place, but she never was sent.

"It was such a difficult time for all the Sisters in Latin America," agreed Sister Arlene Einwalter of Milwaukee, a member of Sister María Rosa's novitiate class of '49. "The governments really didn't want anyone helping the poor." Einwalter had been scheduled to travel to Central America in the mid-1980s, but was held back in Milwaukee because of death squads targeting liberation theologians in Latin America. "What María Rosa achieved, in those days, in that country, against those odds, was so unlikely," she said. "It speaks miracle to me."

Brenner described the intensity of the daily challenges she witnessed her friend tackle—work that might have benefitted from a larger community of women with whom to live and talk things over. On one visit, Sister María Rosa took Brenner into the village home of some very physically and mentally challenged children. One child was retching on a mat on the floor, and a teenage girl lay motionless on a bed. Sister María Rosa sat down gently on the bed and lightly touched the girl on the arm.

"María Rosa said that when she first came to the home, the girl would scream if anyone touched her; the child was an outcast and had never been held or touched," Brenner said. "María Rosa told me, 'Every day we give this girl one touch. Day after day, just one touch. This is the way you can love people into change.'"

When people asked Sister María Rosa about difficult days and years, she said a lot of learning comes from the things that go wrong rather than right, from missteps rather than victory. "No matter what happens, it is never a failure; it's just training," she explained. "If one way isn't too good, God will stop you in some way, somehow, and with somebody to turn you around to the right thing."

Which is what happened several years after Father Willie's death, when SAN experienced a complete about-face as an organization. Sister María Rosa's diverse outreach programs—her freelancing outside the lines of strictly serving orphans under the age of 13—finally led to a break with S.O.S. Kinderdorf and the hundreds of children's homes in their SAN Aldeas S.O.S. alliance. For years S.O.S. founder Hermann Gmeiner had trusted Sister María Rosa's local wisdom in Honduras and looked the other way when she began programs for teenagers, single mothers, handicapped children, the elderly, rural clinics, even farming and selling vegetables to support the poor. After Gmeiner died in 1986, though, his successor at S.O.S., Helmut Kutin, decided to rein in Sister María Rosa's broader efforts.

"The bylaws of S.O.S. said we couldn't have children past the primary grades," said SAN board member Doña Regina Aguilar de Paz. "Over in Europe, S.O.S. sent them to trade schools but we didn't do that here. Sister María Rosa built some trade shops, but S.O.S. didn't like that, even though Hermann Gmeiner liked Honduras—and Sister Maria Rosa —in general. He would always say, 'They have projects for every problem!'"

Sister María Rosa knew that in Honduras, the trenches of poverty were not populated with parentless orphans in a legal sense. Honduras was not a war zone where children's parents were killed, like Nicaragua or El Salvador or even Europe after World War II. Here the need was greater and the risk higher with abandoned and neglected children, street kids, kids living inside prison with their mothers, young adults without education or job training, and the children of unwed or unsupported mothers.

The story goes that Kutin tried to tell Sister María Rosa that she could no longer start new projects or receive children without his permission. "You are not the president of Honduras," he told her.

"And I am not your employee," Sister María Rosa retorted. "I became a religious to work for the children of my country, and here I am at the service of their needs. My vocation, which God gave me when I was six years old, is different than yours. I can't be saying, Help these orphaned children, but not these other people. And I am sorry, but the man who will give me orders is not in this world!"

With that exchange, she walked away from a 20-year relationship with S.O.S. Kinderdorf, from all the homes she had managed in partnership with them, and from an annual funding of nearly $500,000. Some of SAN's current directors raised by Sister María Rosa reported that the Honduran media did not treat her kindly in the split, claiming there were irregularities with financial accounting, another weight to bear at the time. Yet Sister María Rosa did not waver from her trademark tenacity to God's plan. "This work is my vocation," she said. "It was given to me by God and the Blessed Mother, and I wouldn't sell my vocation for 10 million lempiras a year. I could say no to S.O.S., but I could not say no to God."

A lot of older kids from the SAN-S.O.S. alliance, especially from the homes in Tegucigalpa and Zamoranito, chose to leave the S.O.S. projects and go with Sister María Rosa, no matter how uncertain SAN's future might be. She already had a group of young men living together near her office, studying and working and "learning how to mix with the real *sociedad afuera* (society outside)," she said. "I think this is a time, around age 20, when they really need help. It's not too good for those who leave home before they're ready. They are not good men or women yet."

Some of the youth who stayed in the S.O.S. homes did not fare very well.

"Pretty soon, S.O.S. closed some of the SAN projects that weren't about young children," said Pancho Paz. "They closed Zamoranito, the clinics and the teen programs, and made some kids go back with their families if they weren't orphans. Most of the kids from that time say as adults, 'Sister María Rosa is my mother,' even if they were raised in S.O.S. homes."

As SAN found itself in flux, Sister María Rosa said she asked God to show her what to do. She resolved to start SAN over from scratch. "Whatever wasn't working well, the Lord is so good to stop me and have me make this change," she said. "Life has a lot of teaching if you take the time to see it and think and pray."

Sister María Rosa was already experienced in rolling with the punches and even the tragedies. She drew on her own female aptitude for changing direction, and paused to reflect on her work, consulting her Lord in prayer at every turn. Ultimately, Sister María Rosa responded to this call to reorganize like a mother or caregiver rather than a CEO. She decided to return to what she knew best: creating safe homes for the poor. She just grew the idea a little larger this time. She would build a complete rural village where single mothers could make a home, raise and educate their children, work to make a living, and lead a life of dignity.

"So I told the Blessed Mother, 'Here I am, I am ready. I will take care of your poor,'" Sister María Rosa remembered. "I felt ready to do all the things for the kids all over again. I think the Blessed Mother has always been my biggest strength. There is so much to learn from that little girl. To go to Calvary... where did she get that strength? She can give it to us because she has the experience. Just to stay here after the big problem with S.O.S. Kinderdorf and after Father Willie was killed—you cannot do that alone. But the Blessed Mother was with me. She was a woman, too. I don't know if any man could live through all that she did. Sometimes I think that's why Saint Joseph died before Jesus was crucified!"

Father Willie Arsenault

PROFILE: THE NICARAGUAN REFUGEE WHO MANAGED A BRICK FACTORY

Guillermo José Matus Castellón

Guillermo José Matus Castellón still wonders how Sister María Rosa, against all odds, was able to find and rescue him from a Honduran jail during the Nicaraguan Contra war of the 1980s. He and eight other Nicaraguan boys were fleeing military service for the Sandinistas when the hired coyote smuggling them across the border into Honduras got them lost for three days without food and water. Honduran police found them and held them in custody to send back to Nicaragua. The other eight boys were from SAN Aldeas S.O.S. homes in Nicaragua under the care of a woman from Europe who

had arranged to send them to Sister María Rosa in Tegucigalpa and sponsor their education. Matus, known in SAN circles as Chocho, was just tagging along.

Military service in Nicaragua was obligatory for men at age 18, but both the Sandinistas and the Contras were grabbing younger boys off the streets and away from their families. When Chocho was 16, his father sent him to live at his grandparents' house, hoping to spare his son from early service in the army and the war. When the military sent a letter to his father's home looking for him, Chocho went further into hiding, quitting high school and moving into a house with other young men. Padre Rafael María Fibretto, an Italian priest working with the poor in Nicaragua, would visit the boys at the home. Chocho said he was "a little bored" without school, so Fibretto found some work for him. He learned to fix clocks and watches, and then Fibretto took him to work with a man who repaired refrigerators and air conditioners. Chocho gave much of the money he earned to Fibretto because the priest was helping him and the other boys.

At some point, Chocho asked the priest whether there might be someplace to go where he could try to make a better life for himself. Fibretto was already arranging to send the SAN Aldeas S.O.S. boys to Sister María Rosa in Honduras, and the priest asked Chocho if he would like to go with them. "He told me not to tell anybody ahead of time, that he would let me know the day we were going to leave," said Chocho.

On August 26, 1984, Fibretto brought the nine boys to the Honduran border at 3 p.m. and passed them off to the coyote. This man knew a route to get them across the border, but he forgot the way, Chocho said, and they were lost for three days in the forest. "We had no food and no water, and we were close to a place where we knew there were grenades," Chocho recalled. "We would have to take steps in the same places we saw others walk through."

Eventually they stumbled into the Honduran town of San Marcos de Colón, just over the border northeast of Choluteca. Afraid and hungry, they went to the local police. They weren't arrested but they were held in custody. People from the community brought food to the starving boys; they knew the kids were from Nicaragua, fleeing the war. The coyote had headed back to Nicaragua, but Chocho said the people in San Marcos de Colón told Nicaraguan police about him, and the man was killed in the mountains walking back to Nicaragua.

The boys gave false names to the police, afraid they might be turned back to Nicaragua. So when Sister María Rosa called the Minister of Security, looking for eight—not nine—boys sent days ago by Padre Fibretto, none of the names matched.

"Sister was sending a lot of her people to the area, looking for these boys, but she wasn't finding them quickly because the names were wrong from what Padre Fibretto had told her," remembered *Pancho Paz, who was raised in SAN and works for the organization today. "So they were in jail for a day or two until finally one of Sister's men showed the boys a ring he wore that had the shape of the SAN-S.O.S. logo and they recognized it. So Sister knew those were the boys."*

The next day the boys were moved to one small room in a prison in Choluteca; they were considered revolutionaries with no ties to Honduras. The day after that Sister María Rosa herself came to the Choluteca prison, bringing hamburgers for all. Because the boys' names did not match her list, she had trouble convincing the police that these young men were her charges. Through her connections with the Honduran army, she eventually got the boys moved to "a friend's place that was kind of like an orphanage," Chocho said.

"All the boys who met her wanted to go with her after that, even a tenth Nicaraguan guy we met in prison," he continued. "She waited until 10 p.m. and then took us all away from that place. We got to

Miraflores the next day and there were two big pots of chicken soup there for us. We ate everything!"

Schooling for the eight SAN Aldeas S.O.S. boys was already sponsored by the woman who had cared for them, but Sister María Rosa paid for Chocho's education herself. He helped in SAN's Tegucigalpa projects doing repair work and maintenance, worked with Father Willie at SAN's Zamoranito farm, and over the years studied many technical trades (electrical work, welding, air-conditioning) at INFOP, the National Institute for Professional Formation.

"All the other boys eventually went back to Nicaragua," said Paz. "Chocho was the only one who stayed in Honduras, even though he had no family here. He is a great handyman and can repair anything and everything. Every single problem we have, we look for him to fix it. When he moved out to Nuevo Paraíso he was in charge of our brick factory for many years. He built a new water tower in Nuevo, too. The way he made the plans to raise the tank was amazing!"

Today Chocho has a grown daughter, who is a teacher, and two grown sons; one studied in Mexico and works at a large hardware business in Tegucigalpa, and the other is an electrical engineer who is working in Tegucigalpa while he makes plans to pursue a master's degree in project management.

"When I was young, I didn't think a lot about what was happening and what Sor María Rosa did for me," he said. "Now, as an adult, I see her as an angel, because she was waiting for me to give me an education and a life of working here in Honduras. If not for her my family probably wouldn't exist. Or maybe I would have had to try to go to the United States illegally."

Chocho's youngest son, Daniel, known as Chochito ("little Chocho") agreed. "If she wasn't interested in helping people and helping my father, I wouldn't exist," he said. "Sor María Rosa is such a good example of what people can do with their lives. I don't know anyone else like her in Honduras!"

Daniel attributes his own opportunity to study electrical engineering at the national university to the education Sister María Rosa gave his father.

"*We are living in a poor country where a lot of people don't have access to education,*" *he said.* "*Sometimes we need just one opportunity to go, to move forward. Sor María Rosa gave that to people.*"

CHAPTER 8

NEW PARADISE

SISTER MARÍA ROSA CREATES A RURAL VILLAGE FOR SINGLE MOTHERS AND THEIR CHILDREN

--"I ask the Lord that one day there will be no child without a home and a family, no child without food, no child without a way to be trained and go to school and get ready to live in this world. This world is very hard to live in unless you have all that."--

In the wake of SAN's split with S.O.S. Kinderdorf, Sister María Rosa stoked the fire of her vocation with prayer, enthusiasm, and characteristic chutzpah. She widened her vision, expanding her beneficiaries from children alone to include single mothers and other women who were abused and abandoned by their husbands or their families with no means of support. By giving these women hope and opportunity, she would raise the prospects for their children and give both groups a life of dignity.

In 1989 Sister María Rosa founded a rural village for single mothers and their children in the Morocelí Valley, an hour outside Tegucigalpa, on a thousand-acre plot of land she had been using as a farming co-op. In her new village, called Nuevo Paraíso (New Paradise), mothers would live with their kids in safety, with access to schools, medical care, childcare, spiritual guidance, and even training in trades. She held the first planning meeting onsite under a tree; a tractor had to plow a pathway into the fields to get to it. Then she cleared out some old crops and planted corn. Its sale would raise money for the new project, since she had none after the split with S.O.S. During a 1989 radio telethon to raise money for the poor she exhorted Hondurans to "stop sleeping and get up and go to the bank!" so they could contribute to her new project.

The first residents of Nuevo Paraíso came from Sister María Rosa's home for unwed mothers in Comayagua. These founding women and children helped build their own brick homes. Each house had two bedrooms, a dining room, kitchen, and living room under a tile roof, complete with running water. These women farmed the fields, sold produce to markets, and started microbusinesses in sewing, canning, cooking, baking, carpentry, and brickmaking. They grew pumpkins, ginger, onions, tomatoes, papayas, passion fruit, corn, beans, and sugarcane. They made blackberry, passion-fruit, and papaya jelly. They raised pigs and chickens. Some women started a sewing business, which produced school uniforms, cushions, backpacks, bedding, and tablecloths. Several others trained in woodwork and made furniture, cabinets, and doors for the new homes.

"I began Nuevo Paraíso for the ladies with children, the single mothers that I already had—the ones S.O.S. didn't want me to have," Sister María Rosa explained. "I gave a home to every one of them, and Doctor McCallum's groups from Canada helped me pay for and build those homes. We trained the women to work, though some of them had worked already in Tegucigalpa. These women used to be on the streets. But now they could say they had a house and they were taking good care of their children. Now they could say they were somebody!"

Over the next decade or so, a community materialized in Nuevo Paraíso around 40 or 50 single-mother homes and a small neighborhood for married couples. The village grew to include an elementary school serving more than 150 kids (some attended from outside the village), a kindergarten, a high school, a clinic, a bakery, a plantain-chip factory, a cafeteria, and other small businesses. The mothers of the village received education not just in trades and microenterprises, but in maternal responsibilities, spiritual formation, and caring for a home. Their crops were very successful: Nuevo Paraíso was feeding its own families and selling truckloads of tomatoes to other villages as far away as El Salvador. A clinic at Nuevo Paraíso offered medical services for the village's residents, and Sister María Rosa's new Apostoles de la Salud (Apostles of Health) program brought health care into rural areas; its doctors served a monthly average of 1,800 to 2,000 people. A new brick factory employed about 20 mothers and children. By 1998, the village of Nuevo Paraíso had a population of more than 300.

In late October 1998, disaster arrived in a terrifyingly familiar form. The deadliest Atlantic storm in 200 years, Hurricane Mitch, swirled into a Category 5 monster with sustained winds of 180 miles per hour. It stalled off the north coast of Honduras for several devastating days before it made landfall, weakened, and drifted south across the country. Three to six feet of rain were dumped on Honduras and Nicaragua by the slow-moving storm. The new international airport in San Pedro Sula, Honduras's second-largest city, was submerged and rivers overflowed. The Choluteca River in Tegucigalpa rose 10 meters above its banks.

In Honduras the damage went far beyond the storm surge and hurricane-force winds. The extensive rainfall triggered flooding in mountainous terrain, causing mudslides and other catastrophes. No international death toll was ever established due to the chaos and massive damages, but in Honduras death estimates ranged from 7,000 to 11,000 people. Rural mountain communities suffered the most: Slash-and-burn agriculture had left the forests and farmland unable to absorb the storm's moisture, thus water simply cascaded down the hillsides to flood villages, bury roads, drown residents, and isolate survivors behind landslides and washouts. Others succumbed to the cholera, dengue fever, and malaria that spread when clean water became scarce. After the storm, about 70 percent of the population had no drinkable water.

Three-fourths of the country's infrastructure—bridges, roads, electricity, water, sanitation—was wiped out. Flooding affected more than a third of Honduras's farmable land; 90 percent of the banana crop, the main export, was destroyed. About a million Hondurans were left homeless. Damage to schools, hospitals, roads, farms, homes, and businesses was estimated at $3.8 billion. President Carlos Roberto Flores claimed that Honduras's economy and progress had been set back 50 years.

SAN was crushed by the storm, as well. Many of Sister María Rosa's buildings and the homes of her employees or their families were destroyed. Most of SAN's farms, crops, and businesses were ravaged like everyone else's; their agriculture program has not recovered to this day.

"I lost all my tomatoes, green peppers, plantains, and papayas," Sister María Rosa recalled. "The plantains were for the ladies making plantain chips—for their business. And I used to love selling the tomatoes to El Salvador because I felt like we were the poor supporting the poor with our own business. I could have gone to Canada to ask our friends for money for food, and I knew I would get it, but I didn't want to do it that way; I preferred to have our own crops. Now they were gone and all that was left was to borrow money."

For Sister María Rosa and SAN, however, recovery wouldn't take anywhere near the 50 years Flores predicted for the country. From her involvement with Hurricane Fifi and several earthquakes in neighboring countries, Sister María Rosa was very experienced in mobilizing people and gathering resources in frantic post-disaster settings. When the Honduran government turned relief efforts over to the churches and religious organizations, SAN was poised to become a front-line relief agency for storm victims. Humanitarian aid poured in immediately—the United States gave Honduras more than $460 million in disaster funds from 1998 to 2001. During this time, Sister María Rosa coordinated efforts from UNICEF and other humanitarian groups to distribute food, clothing, water, and medicine directly to survivors. SAN, the School Sisters of Saint Francis, a group called Hands to Honduras, and other organizations formed medical brigades to dig their way into isolated rural communities and bring help.

Jim McCallum, who was in Tegucigalpa at a soccer game when Hurricane Mitch made landfall on the north coast, reluctantly took the last commercial flight out of Honduras during the storm. Sister María Rosa had insisted that he go, telling him that he could help her more from Canada. From home he sent many container loads of donated relief supplies, plus money to build a large storage warehouse near Sister María Rosa's Miraflores office compound.

McCallum flew back to Honduras three months after the storm. Sister María Rosa had completed the warehouse, but had a new idea—a temporary use—for the building other than storage.

"As a grand opening for the warehouse, she hosted an Epiphany dinner for the homeless and the drunks of Tegucigalpa," McCallum said. "She wanted to provide food, healthcare, and clothing to all the people living on the streets—so many more since the hurricane. She asked the Honduran Army to round up all these men from the city streets. This might not have been such a good idea, since some people remembered being conscripted into military service by officers grabbing them like that. A lot of men ran away at first. But when they found out that Sister María Rosa was behind it, they came."

The warehouse was decorated and a big meal was ready. McCallum said the men were told they had to stand in line for a medical checkup outside the warehouse before going in. Tensions rose as all of these hungry homeless men waited to eat until everyone was inside.

"Some of them were pretty mean-looking characters, and we were nervous," McCallum remembered. "Things were about to explode when Sister María Rosa finally walked into the room. She had such a calming effect on everybody: Suddenly everyone was happy. Sister sat in the middle of all these destitute men and ate with them. The rest of us had trouble getting past the smell of these people, but she was in her glory with them."

Sister María Rosa recalled that day. "Doctor McCallum

was our photographer and our master of ceremonies," she reported. "I chose Epiphany for when the wise men came to Bethlehem, and I told those men that each of them has a star to follow. I said, 'If you drink too much, you are just looking down. You have to stop drinking to look up and find your star!'"

Sister María Rosa continued the tradition of the Epiphany dinner for several years. She also started a medical clinic downtown to serve the alcoholics and the homeless who lived by the market and cemetery. Pancho Paz's mother, Moncha (Ramona), staffed the clinic as a nurse twice a week for many years. These short-term projects widened the scope of SAN's ministry: Besides women and children, Sister María Rosa was now serving homeless and alcoholic men.

"Jesus was homeless, too, you know," she was fond of concluding whenever she told this story.

Long after the international relief organizations went home, SAN remained a primary source of aid to hurricane victims. Several months after Mitch, Sister María Rosa donated to storm victims one of her remaining assets: land. She gave away a large portion of the Nuevo Paraíso property to help solve Honduras's extreme homelessness following the hurricane. An international organization called Nuestros Pequeños Hermanos (Our Little Brothers and Sisters) built 200 homes there for all the people living in tents in the fields nearby. Today, that village is called Nueva Esperanza (New Hope). It has its own churches and businesses, and many current SAN employees live there.

"I happened to be back in Honduras at the meeting where Sister gave away the land for the new houses," said McCallum. "There were all these officials there from both church and government—government agencies, Cardinal

Rodriguez, and I think even a representative from Rome—all sitting at Sister's dining room table forming post-Mitch reconstruction plans for the poor."

Sister María Rosa insisted on donating, not selling, her land. "I just gave away the land," she said. "I didn't charge them anything for it. I have no time for dealing with that. God will take care of all that."

Reconstruction after Mitch was for many years an epic slog through mud, debris, and enormous losses. The earliest mission groups to come to work at SAN found complete devastation in Tegucigalpa, a full 15 months after the hurricane. From the vantage point of Cristo del Picacho, the new Christ statue overlooking the city from 4,353 feet above sea level, mission travelers could see miles of hillside gouged or stripped away. Four blocks of homes and offices on either side of the Choluteca River were wiped out. Roads and bridges were washed away and everything felt "migratory and transient," said Phyllis Stewart-Hope, a January 2000 mission traveler from Immaculate Heart of Mary parish in Indianapolis. "There was just utter devastation in Tegucigalpa, but then we went out to Nuevo Paraíso and there was action: hundreds of white tents lined up in the area that would become Nueva Esperanza."

Rural Nuevo Paraíso felt to visitors like an oasis of hope compared with the disaster areas in the rest of Honduras. "In Tegucigalpa, the devastation was just overwhelming," said Beth Murphy, another member of that January 2000 mission team. "But when we got out to Nuevo Paraíso, it was kind of refreshing. There was a feeling of newness, like this was an answer, a problem being solved. Sister was a rescuer, and we were going to get to help. The beauty was that it wasn't too big or too organized. The fun was in developing it all alongside her."

In the midst of so much adversity and despair, Sister María Rosa was to visitors a rock of confidence in the future of SAN and her children's village at Nuevo Paraíso. Shirley Ahlrichs, from the Indianapolis group, told a story about Sister María Rosa coming out from Tegucigalpa to visit the mission group guests who were painting the village chapel. The single mothers who lived in Nuevo Paraíso were helping, lending their brooms to help extend the paint brushes to reach the high places.

"Sister María Rosa stood on the altar and told us for the first time the story of SAN," Ahlrichs remembered. "One of us asked her whether she had seen or heard from any of those young people she had raised in the sixties and seventies. And she just reached out to Pancho Paz standing with her and said, 'Here is one of them.' Then she pointed to Carlos Rene Caceres: 'Here is another.' And then Quique Rodriguez. And then Dania Hernandez. She told us, 'These people you see working so hard here as directors were raised here. They are my children!'"

෯෨෯

AROUND THE TIME HURRICANE RELIEF SLOWED DOWN FOR SAN, Nuevo Paraíso began to show signs of trouble as a community. Some of the single mothers had psychological or emotional issues that were too significant for SAN's expertise or resources; some were unfit to care for their children. Others were good mothers, but chafed against the rules forbidding them from bringing men into their homes. Sister María Rosa found it difficult to change the stories of single mothers who continued to have more babies when they couldn't care for the children they already had.

"It felt right to keep families—these women and their children—together in theory," McCallum remembered. "But in practical terms, we discovered after a while that some of the mothers needed tremendous psychological help. It was really difficult to build good relationships among them."

So McCallum and Sister María Rosa discussed changing direction again. They decided to revert back to Sister María Rosa's original mission and populate the Nuevo Paraíso homes with children rather than single mother families. Sister María Rosa modeled these new Nuevo Paraíso children's homes after her SAN homes in Tegucigalpa, with small family groups of 10 to 12 kids and a housemother in each house. There was no shortage of children in need: abandoned kids, orphaned kids, kids with parents in jail, plus the kids whose Nuevo Paraíso mothers were unable to care for them. Another benefit to changing the project: It would be easier to solicit sponsorship for children alone than to raise funds for single mothers. Sister María Rosa believed that First World nations could help Honduras by helping its children, and the new teams of mission travelers loved to play with the SAN kids.

"We started our first new children's home, Roswindis House, with eight children from two mothers who had to leave Nuevo Paraíso," remembered Mae Valenzuela, SAN's director of volunteers. "The day they left was very sad. But we promised those mothers we would take care of their kids. Then we started the second house after María Faustina, one of the single mothers, died and left three kids. Three other girls of a mother with psychological problems came to live there, too."

The healthy families at Nuevo Paraíso with capable mothers moved out on their own into brand-new homes nearby in Barrio Santiago and Nueva Esperanza. SAN made a down payment on each family's house, and the women worked to pay for and eventually own their homes. "They'd pay the mortgage down with about $10 a month," McCallum said. "There are so many success stories from that first group; many of the children of these original women eventually went to university."

One of those single mothers who moved with her children first to Nuevo Paraíso and then out to Santiago has put three sons through college. Teresa Gomez owns a plantain-chip factory in Nueva Esperanza, which Sister María Rosa helped her start in Nuevo Paraíso first. The shop has been Gomez' independent business since 2009. "When I used to live in Tegucigalpa, I cared for an old lady. But she died and I was out of a job," said Gomez. "Someone recommended me to Sister María Rosa so I could stay with my three sons, and we moved to Nuevo Paraíso."

In Nuevo Paraíso, Gomez said, she felt safe like never before. "Sister's mission was to instruct us to 'be somebody in life,' and she said we had to be trained before we could own our own businesses," she said. "I started my shop with one stove and one table, selling about 10 plantains a day. Now I am selling to big stores and schools, including the agricultural school at Zamorano. Now I have a government permit and a health registry." The success of her business allowed her to send all her children to university, where two studied computer science and one studied marketing.

"Sister María Rosa was like a great mother who has never given birth to a child," Gomez declared. "She was a tough lady, and when she had to spank you she would. But when you needed a hug, she would do that, too. All I can say is, What would I be today if Sister didn't start Nuevo Paraíso?"

Sister María Rosa directs Hurricane Mitch cleanup efforts

PROFILE: THE SELF-MADE BEVERLY HILLS PARALEGAL WHO BECAME ABUELA TO HUNDREDS OF CHILDREN

Mae Patricia Cruz Valenzuela

SAN's hostess for mission groups once earned a whopping amount of money in Los Angeles, living it up in high style with a white Mercedes and an apartment in Brentwood. Born in Honduras, niece of a former president and also of SAN's cofounder, Reyes Irene Valenzuela, Mae Patricia Cruz Valenzuela had escaped the random violence of Tegucigalpa around age 20 to live for awhile in California and learn English as her sisters and cousins had done. When her sisters got married in the United States, she ended up staying for more than 30 years.

As a young adult, Valenzuela worked days in a Beverly Hills law office and attended Los Angeles City College and UCLA at night. She brought in so many Hispanic clients to the law firm that she became quite rich from referral money. She expected to live out her days in California, but two unexpected things happened: First, she came back to Honduras temporarily to fulfill a promise, and second, she stayed.

In her forties while living in California, Valenzuela said she had several mystical visions of an eye, a symbol of wisdom, that made her believe that God was urging her to change her life. During a 1990 pilgrimage to the site of Marian apparitions in Medjugorje, in Bosnia and Herzegovina, Valenzuela witnessed the sun dancing in pulsing silver and rainbow colors and later saw lights flashing high in Saint James Church when the apparition started there. At that point, she said, she could smell a thousand roses, even though her sinuses were very congested at the time. Then she received what she called a "great gift from Our Lady"—a piercing pain that felt like a heart attack at first, but eventually subsided.

"I think she gave me the pain so I would have strength to help my mother die in prayer the next year," Valenzuela concluded.

Later, on Apparition Hill, Valenzuela came upon the Honduran flag of blue stars on white, draped over rocks on the side of the pathway. She took it as a sign from the Blessed Mother that she should think about Honduras.

Visits to California in 1994 and 1998 by an increasingly frail Aunt Reyes convinced Valenzuela it was time to fulfill a promise she had made to her dying mother: to come home to Honduras to be company for Valenzuela's aging, daughterless aunts when they were close to the end of their lives. She planned to return to her high life in Los Angeles after Reyes passed away. Arriving in Honduras in June 1998, Valenzuela set about organizing Reyes's house—the Christmas tree was still up—and lining up work to teach English in a new project with international NGO Save the Children. That job would have started November 1, but Hurricane Mitch made land-

fall in Honduras in late October. Save the Children decided to cancel her project and use the funds for relief.

Two weeks after the hurricane, Sister María Rosa called Valenzuela to ask if she would lead a SAN medical brigade into a rural area hit hard by Mitch. The way Sister María Rosa told the story, she was relieving Valenzuela of the duty of cleaning mud off the walls of her aunt's flooded home.

"She did not want to come to SAN," Sister María Rosa liked to say. "When her aunts used to tell her she should go work with me, Mae would say no, she could not see herself working for SAN!"

But she did go, and that first brigade made a strong impact.

"We had to cross the river on a rope and we almost drowned!" Valenzuela recalled. "We went in open trucks lent to Sister by the Army, and the roads were so bad. We took water, clothing, food, and medicine. On that brigade, I saw what Honduras was really like—I had forgotten the terrible poverty, how poor my people were. I made a decision then that I would stay in Honduras, not just for my aunt. I would work for Sociedad. It was five years after my Aunt Reyes died before I even went back to L.A. to visit. But I hated the freeways and crowds in California then. I had promised some of the mothers in our projects here that I would watch over their kids, and I couldn't wait to leave L.A. and come back to the children."

"I think Mae was always supposed to be in this office, working with the American and Canadian groups, translating, doing all kinds of things," Sister María Rosa told me. "She is excellent with the groups; nobody can do what she is doing, and she has made a lot of friends for us."

Today the former Californian facilitates and coordinates travel, accommodations, meals, brigades, translators, souvenir shopping, and even birthday cakes for the North American mission groups. Valenzuela is the welcoming hug at the airport, the go-to person for every question, the gateway face and voice of SAN to many North Amer-

ican volunteers. She is also known as Abuela *[Grandma] Apple to hundreds of SAN children, whom she showers with hugs, kisses, apples, and intimate attention to their needs. This is a family that Valenzuela, who biologically cannot have children, never thought she would have.*

Valenzuela is 100 percent convinced that she is on track with God's plan now. "Before I came here, God would take things away, like my good health or my desire to make money in business," she said. "In that period of my life, I always felt, 'What is my purpose?' But here I finally feel fulfilled in a way I didn't feel even with money and material things. These children need me. If I have had even a little to do with their good futures and successes, I feel that my life is not being wasted. I want to be a grandma to these kids for as long as the Lord allows me."

She also feels that Sister María Rosa helped point her in the direction of God's plan for her life, even if Valenzuela initially came to Honduras against her will.

"But then I chose to stay," she smiled. "She was my mentor, teacher, and guide. I laughed with her, I cried with her, I prayed with her, I argued with her, I learned from her. I remember when we received 15 babies at one time in Nuevo Paraíso and I was worried about how we would care for them. She told me, 'Woman of little faith, are they your children? No. Are they my children? No. They are God's. Trust that He will take care of them.' And then the groups started to buy diapers and big cans of formula and Pediasure nutrition, so that soon I had a storeroom of things for the babies.

"Because of Sister I have my faith. I hated to get up early but did it willingly at 3 a.m. just to pray with Sister. It gave me peace and moved me. When I was praying with her I had the feeling that God was listening so closely!"

PROFILE: THE PATRIARCH WHO MAKES ANNUAL FIX-IT TRIPS TO HONDURAS

Larry Hildebrand

Larry Hildebrand, of Osh Kosh, Wisconsin, said he felt a momentous push from God to come to Honduras for the first time. It was early 1999 and the aftermath of Hurricane Mitch's destruction still dominated the world news. Hildebrand was watching a TV program showing terrible flooding and people being washed down rivers. Right then, his grown son called home and asked, "Dad, are you watching TV? Do you see what's going on in Honduras?" Surprised that they were both watching the same show, they agreed, "We should do something to try to help."

Hildebrand contacted the School Sisters of Saint Francis in Milwaukee to ask how his family might help hurricane victims in

Central America. The Sisters described what Sister María Rosa was doing for children in Tegucigalpa and rural Honduras; they said she would know a lot of people struggling to rebuild after the storm. They also told Hildebrand that his talents would be in very high demand in post-Mitch Honduras. His career was in servicing electronics; he and his wife ran an apartment rental business, so they were eminently handy with construction, plumbing, and rebuilding.

"So we just bought plane tickets for Honduras," Hildebrand said. "We left Wisconsin on January 6, 1999. First we toured Tegucigalpa and saw the terrible state of things everywhere. Then we got out to Nuevo Paraíso. The Canadian government had just sent these large commercial water purifiers, so we installed them for Sister and her people. We were so glad we could do something right away to help."

On that first trip, the Hildebrands saw busloads of displaced Hondurans coming from Tegucigalpa out to the Nuevo Paraíso area to look at property for a new settlement—land where they might build a new home.

"This was right when Sister María Rosa gave away her land near Nuevo Paraíso for homeless people to build new houses," Hildebrand says. "We ended up doing the wiring for the machines that made cement blocks. Those machines would make two big blocks every 15 minutes or so. We kept two machines running 24 hours a day to make blocks to build the new houses in what would be Nueva Esperanza."

The following year the Hildebrands came back and wired the Nuevo Paraíso school for electricity.

"Then we just kept coming, once or twice a year, for several weeks at a time, to do whatever was needed," Hildebrand said.

In his eighties, Hildebrand still travels to Honduras. His retinue of family and friends bring expert experience in wiring, plumbing, and construction to help build, maintain, and renovate SAN's homes and schools. They even wired electricity out to the kitchen, dormi-

tory, and other buildings at SAN's Flor Azul farm. Back home in Wisconsin, they continue to raise funds for SAN and collect gifts and supplies for Sister María Rosa's children.

As a frequent visitor to SAN and Nuevo Paraíso, Hildebrand has witnessed the occasional traveler who just doesn't get it, who is frustrated with the Honduran way of doing things or with not completing a project during their weeklong mission trip.

"The good intentions of Americans can sometimes get out of hand," he said. He laughed about a man who once asked him why Sister didn't just pour blacktop all over Nuevo Paraíso and rent out golf carts for people to get around. Hildebrand said he enjoys the "aha" moment that comes to most members of his team—usually four or five days into the trip. "It's so good to bring friends down and watch them realize how happy people can be here, to let them see Honduran people satisfied with so little," Hildebrand smiled.

The biggest draw in Honduras, at least to Hildebrand, was always Sister María Rosa herself.

"From the very first year, even right after the hurricane, we found that Sister María Rosa had such a positive attitude," he said. "She would always say, God will provide, and through the years that has been an inspiration to us. She did struggle financially. But she always trusted that God would provide."

Hildebrand showed me a photograph he carries of Sister María Rosa holding up a framed cross-stitching of SAN's motto: There Is Always Room for One More.

"She made us better people," he continued. "She made us so much more aware of what's going on in Honduras and in the Third World. And it's been so great to see those SAN kids grow up over the years. Not every story is a success, but some large percentage certainly is. Some kids who came to her had terrible lives, terrible histories. It's neat to see them become great young people. What SAN is doing will make a better country and a better world. Their country has real

problems, and without what Sister gave them, where would those kids be?"

Hildebrand will continue to travel down to Honduras with his team of handy men and women as long as he can. He said that this is his calling, and he finds the work perfectly suited to his family's expertise, talents, and desires.

"I definitely think that God called us to use our skills to go work with Sister María Rosa," he said. "Why else would our son call at the very moment we were watching on TV what was happening in Honduras? Through that, we got our connection with Sister, and we are so blessed to still be able to do the work."

CHAPTER 9

THE JEWELS IN SAN'S CROWN

SISTER MARÍA ROSA CREATES DIVERSE AND LASTING PROGRAMS TO SERVE HONDURANS AT RISK

--"Love one another, the saying goes. But I say to you: Rub on one another. That's how you feel the needs of others—when you hug someone who smells of sweat, or has no clothes, or even when you get all muddy yourself from mixing cement to fix the children's houses. That's how you love one another."--

Except for the Nuevo Paraíso village of children's homes, SAN's current and most wide-reaching projects were all founded at the start of the 21st century. Sister María Rosa launched each program simply, without any grand scheme or master plan, in response to urgent needs among her own children and the Honduran poor. In the early 2000s, she diversified SAN's outreach with a large rural medical clinic, new children's homes for urban street kids in Tegucigalpa, an education project for young female domestic workers, a farm school for teenage boys, and more microbusinesses for her grown children. In addition, she gave away land for a hospice for kids with HIV and AIDS. Her penchant for creating projects wherever she saw a need, regardless of SAN's finances, was bolstered by confidence in past successes. It's likely she would have embarked upon these projects anyway, though, with or without prior success.

"Sometimes it's hard for people to understand the way she thought, and the fact that she always said, 'Don't worry about things, God will provide,'" said Pancho Paz. "It's how she worked. She just started things and then afterward found a way to pull them off."

SANTA ROSA DE LIMA CLINIC (2000)

On Sister María Rosa's 74th birthday, SAN opened the Santa Rosa de Lima Clinic, named in honor of its founder, a short distance from the children's homes at Nuevo Paraíso. Until then, medical care in the village had been housed in one of the original brick homes.

"It was really just a run-down green and yellow house. I saw the nurse chase rats out of the building," remembered Jim McCallum. "There was no clinic in the entire area, so they were doing a lot of medical stuff out of that tiny house."

Built through the generosity of Daniel Meehan, a Milwaukee philanthropist, with support from Rotarians and Friends of Honduran Children Canada, the clinic opened in November 2000 with an emergency department, pharmacy, laboratory, examination rooms, a two-chair dental wing, and labor and delivery services. Soon the clinic added an ambulance. For many years Meehan sent six or seven 40-foot shipping containers filled with medical equipment and other supplies annually to equip the clinic. Jim McCallum also sent funds and supplies from Canada, as did several medical centers in the United States.

"I grew up working in La Policlínica hospital, so I believe that you have to provide health care for people," Sister María Rosa declared. "They do need education and chances to learn how to work, but first they need health to have a good life."

With the only 24-hour emergency room in the region, the Santa Rosa de Lima Clinic immediately provided affordable health care to a large rural population. In its early days a consultation with a doctor cost less than $2. For many years the clinic was home to a Cuban government program called Miracle Mission, which provided eye surgery and care for other eye diseases. When she found out that the Cuban constitution required medical graduates to give two years of service overseas in exchange for free tuition, a savvy Sister María Rosa asked her Cuban contacts to send five doctors and a dentist annually to work at her clinic. These doctors performed more than 70 laser eye surgeries every day on patients who came from all over Central America.

Meehan supported the clinic through a roller-coaster ride of changes and developments over many years. Some were improvements, like two expansions and reclassification as a full-fledged hospital in 2008. Others were catastrophic, like right after the 2009 government coup, when all the Cuban doctors left in the night, pulling their equipment out of the walls to take with them. The clinic had to close. In 2012 the clinic was renovated and relaunched under the Honduran Ministry of Health and operates today with an emergency room, obstetrics and labor department, inpatient rooms, and a lab for blood tests and X-rays. In 2017, the clinic received 10,744 patients and surpassed by 21 births its goal of 300 deliveries. The Ministry of Health pays for these deliveries; other medical services require that patients pay a nominal fee, but care is provided for free if a patient cannot pay.

MONTAÑA DE LUZ (2000)

The Montaña de Luz hospice for children with HIV infection or AIDS was never a formal program of SAN, though many brigade teams who come to Nuevo Paraíso assume so and there has been some overlap with volunteers. Sister María Rosa is sometimes credited with starting the project because she gave the mission her blessing and its home in the village of Nueva Esperanza: a beautiful hilltop property with a panoramic view of the sugarcane fields of the Morocelí Valley. Sister Kathlyn Brenner said that Sister María Rosa also renamed the property Montaña de Luz (Mountain of Light) from Montaña de Duendes (Mountain of Devils or Goblins), its unofficial moniker ever since a local man had seen a vision of oxen dragging a cart filled with dead bodies.

The Montaña de Luz project was founded on November 21, 2000, the same day Santa Rosa de Lima Clinic opened. Honduras at the time had the highest prevalence of HIV and AIDS in the region, with nearly two-thirds of the HIV infections in Central America and more than 70 percent of its AIDS cases. This project was the brainchild of Reverend Russell J. Crabtree, a Presbyterian pastor from Columbus, Ohio, who started Project Heart Strong to serve Honduras's large AIDS population. He built a compound with housing for up to 30 children and staff. In addition to living quarters, it has a dining room, kitchen, study hall, fields for outdoor play, a recreation center, and a chapel. Crabtree's brother-in-law, Duane Knecht, joined in from Michigan and brought a team from his Hands to Honduras program to help the project get started. One team member, AIDS nurse Christine Frederick, came for a year and then stayed for more than a decade as director of the project.

Montaña de Luz was initially conceived as a home where children with AIDS could receive basic nutrition and loving care for the short, sick duration of their lives. As antiretroviral drugs became widely available, however, this home for dying children became a home for children surviving and living to adulthood with AIDS. The directors were faced with the happy challenge of sending these children to school and preparing them for a productive future. In short time, an air-conditioned room designed as a morgue was remodeled into a computer lab for children's homework. Psychologists began working with the children not to prepare them to die, but to help them deal with the death or abandonment of parents and the prejudice they would face in the larger society for being HIV-positive or having AIDS. Because the virus destroys their immune systems, they catch colds and other illnesses easily and often, but the project's tiny cemetery, in which four children were buried in a two-year span, has added only one child grave in the last decade.

"I gave them the place to use," said Sister María Rosa. "All my crazy kids wanted to build me a house up there. But I told them, I will never need a house. Give it to someone who needs it. And then right away some people asked if they could use it to help children with AIDS. And that was good. People and leaders come and go there, but I don't ever tell them what to do."

. . .

REYES IRENE VALENZUELA INSTITUTE (2001)

The Reyes Irene Valenzuela Institute for teenage domestic workers is named after Sister María Rosa's friend and SAN cofounder, who died in January 2001. Against the advice of her board of directors, Sister María Rosa abruptly stopped renting out one of her Tegucigalpa buildings to a bilingual school. Instead, she used that building to respond to a request. An organization from England called Save the Children wanted to sponsor a Tegucigalpa school for street kids, so Sister María Rosa developed a project for a demographic group close to her heart: teenage girls exploited as Tegucigalpa's informal workforce.

In one of the worst abuses of Honduran child labor laws, these young women were typically paid an average of only $40 a month for a six-day workweek of 16-hour days, either as domestic help in private homes or in roadside market stands selling fruit, food, or crafts. Many of them came to Tegucigalpa from the poorest rural communities, sent by a parent who mistakenly thought the girl would be well fed, have a roof over her head, and might enjoy her employer's higher standard of living. Sometimes young girls were given to employers as maids to pay off a family debt. A lot of these working teenagers, separated at a young age from their families, instead became single mothers and victims of sexual abuse or domestic violence behind closed doors, working long hours with little pay or hope for education or a better life. The young women often lost access to school, health care, their families, and any form of recreation or time off.

"Oh, yes, everyone was against this idea at first," remembered Sister María Rosa. "They said, 'How can you give up the 50,000 lempira rent you get from that bilingual school?' And I told them, 'Can you stop and think about 50 or 500 or

5,000 girls that will benefit from this new program? Yes, I need the 50,000 lempira, but if I have 50 girls who can be someone, I can change communities and make a big difference in lives. Nobody respects them when they just work in the homes or on the street. Now some of them have gone on to university!'"

Sister María Rosa contacted a doctor she knew, Liliana Enamorado, to help create an education program for teenage girls. Enamorado and her husband, Javier Zelaya, recruited teachers and the project was launched with 60 girls ages 12 to 18 who worked full-time and came to school on their one day off per week. The young women studied accelerated primary and secondary education, personal hygiene and reproductive health, Honduran labor laws, character formation, music and drama, health, and personal legal rights. They could also study technical and vocational trades in computer repair, hairdressing, paralegal studies, and starting their own businesses.

"Some of those first girls here are through university now," Sister María Rosa proudly reported. "Some had had babies already, some had had an abortion, and they were only 14 or 15 years old. They came in dressed like they were asking for trouble—I told the doctor to give them uniforms so they would look decent. I wanted a big change for them. One girl I remember was forced every day by her mother to bring home a large amount of money; she was a prostitute. Now that girl is working in our project."

Enrollment more than doubled in the second year to 150 girls. Liliana Enamorado's sister, Concepción (Chony) Enamorado, a teacher and civil engineer, soon joined the project and remains the director today. In 2008 the Reyes Irene Valenzuela Institute was selected as one of 20 semifinalists out of 1,200 applicants for the United Nations Economic Commission for Latin America's "Experiences in Social Innovation" prize. One judge noted that "this program deserves to be replicated throughout Central America."

"Most people think this is a school, but it's actually a project to stabilize mentally and physically all of these kids who have experienced extreme abuse or violence in their lives," said Chony Enamorado. "We give them three things: human formation, an academic degree, and a push to go to university or help to find employment."

This remains one of SAN's most successful programs.

"I introduced all kinds of fundraising ideas and grant materials, and Chony took to it like a duck to water," said Jack Licate, retired director of fundraising for the Cleveland Clinic and a close advisor to SAN. "She immediately realized the need for outside fundraising since, as she said, 'We don't have cute children to hug here.' She built budgets, responded to audits, and opened up funding sources in multiple countries that no other project in SAN has been able to."

Since 2003 enrollment has been a consistent 450 girls per year, with 500 on the waiting list. More than 4,000 girls have attended the institute, and about half have gained wage-paying positions. As of July 2015, 80 graduates had moved on to university and 30 had started their own businesses. Four hundred and fifty girls had achieved their high school diplomas. One graduate with a law degree recently came back to volunteer.

The Reyes Irene program is one of Jim McCallum's favorites. His Friends of Honduran Children organization has over the years provided microloans of 100 Canadian dollars to Reyes Irene girls wanting to start their own businesses. "We would go down and interview these girls with the help of the school director," he said. "We'd provide loans of $100 to those with a business plan who are deserving. For instance, one girl was selling peanuts on the city buses. She wanted to buy her own roaster and cut out the middleman who did the roasting for her. By doing that, she was able to expand and hire four or five other girls and pay the money back in about a year."

He laughed about one success story. "There was a girl who had a real entrepreneurial spirit," he said. "She made beautiful clothing and bags to sell and she used the loan money to buy a second sewing machine and hire some girls to work for her. But sometime during that first year of the loan she told us she was upset she had to wait a year to apply for another microloan—she wanted to expand even more right now. I explained that if she could pay off her original loan now, she could get a new one. She had the money already, but thought she had to wait till the end of the year to pay it back!"

Jack Licate remembers hearing a 15-year-old Reyes Irene student give a witness about how the school is changing her life. With her 18-month-old daughter on her hip, she said, "I am here at this school because this baby is not going to have the life I lived before now, the one my mother lived, my grandmother lived. She is going to get an education. Just like I am doing."

PEDRO ATALA HOMES (2002)

After the immense destruction of Hurricane Mitch, homelessness in Tegucigalpa swelled tremendously. Thousands of abandoned children survived in the streets by washing cars at stoplights for a few pennies, searching the

garbage dump for food to eat or items to sell, and begging—
often mandated by adults. Many kids were sexually or physically abused. Others were hooked on drugs or sniffed glue to
combat hunger.

"Families in Tegucigalpa were always asking me for help,
so I got a little push to start some new homes there," Sister
María Rosa said.

So Sister María Rosa renovated several buildings in
SAN's Miraflores office compound into homes for children.
Honduras's government agency for children and families
immediately referred 21 children to SAN and then Sister
María Rosa strode again into prison, this time in the central
Honduran city of Comayagua, to rescue more young children living inside with their incarcerated mothers. She
provided all these Tegucigalpa children the same benefits she
offered in Nuevo Paraíso: a safe home with a housemother,
good food, health care, psychological counseling, and enrollment in local schools.

She named her new project Hogares Don Pedro Atala,
after SAN's first board president. Over the years, the Atala
family's generosity to SAN remains legendary. They continue
to fund some of the needs of the Pedro Atala Homes and
pay for special outings for the children, like swimming and
horseback riding. Today the urban project is home to more
than 50 kids, with an onsite kindergarten, English instructor,
tutors for homework, a computer room, library, and a beautiful chapel.

Much of this project's success—and the achievements of
its grown children—hails from the strong leadership of Sonia
Erazo, its director. Erazo has worked with SAN or S.O.S. ever
since began volunteering at age 16 after school to help care

for the children. She is known by two nicknames: To the children, she is *Tia* (Auntie) Sonia; they love and respect her and come back for visits and advice even after they are grown. To the North American visitors, she is *La Jefa,* the Chief, known for her fierce advocacy for her Pedro Atala children and the tight ship she runs there. There is little turnover in her staff, and the homes are excellently managed with teaching and homework assistance from Santa Elizabeth Cruz Barahona and her sister Rosa, who were raised as children of SAN. The children living in the Pedro Atala homes are well disciplined. They work hard in school and in their English lessons and play hard on a playground and in a new sports center.

Throughout her career, Erazo has fielded job offers from high places, but has repeatedly chosen to stay and partner with Sister María Rosa and SAN. "God knows my work here," she said. "It can be hard to do this work, but if you love my children, then I love you. So many times I was asked to work somewhere else with more money, but I said no. When my grown children come back to me and say, 'Tia Sonia, you helped me,' that is a lot of money for me. That is my pay."

FLOR AZUL YOUTH FARM (2003)

Half a decade after Hurricane Mitch, Sister María Rosa was anxious to get back to growing produce. She was also concerned about the labor exploitation of young people living in the rural areas, with little access to education or a future besides working the fields. In 2004 two young men walked and hitchhiked halfway across the country from the town of Trujillo, on the north coast, to arrive at her door.

They asked her to take them in because they'd heard of her reputation for rescuing children.

"They were from a tribe, and they hardly even spoke Spanish," Sister María Rosa recalled. "They said, 'Somebody told us to look for you and we finally found you. We want to study and learn.' But they were too old and too big to live with the smaller children of Nuevo Paraíso or Pedro Atala."

Around the same time, a man married to one of Sister María Rosa's nieces also arrived, announcing that he would like to do some kind of work for Sister María Rosa now that he had retired from the Standard Fruit Company (Dole).

"I had all the land from Nuevo Paraíso to what is now Flor Azul and I told him there was just an old farmhouse out there but I wanted to start a farm," Sister María Rosa said. "I told him I had two boys already for the farm. Before a week was over I had seven boys!"

Her relative started the Flor Azul (Blue Flower) project with his own money, since SAN had none to spare for the startup. Sister María Rosa recruited more young men to help him. "I went to a pueblo and I found boys there doing nothing," she said. "They couldn't go to school because it was too far away and their fathers wanted them only to work. I thought we could train these boys to grow things beyond beans and corn and also give them an education."

Sister María Rosa hired a teacher and set up a school. The farm quickly became a residential work-study program for poverty-stricken boys from rural Honduras, along with boys from Nuevo Paraíso and the Pedro Atala Homes once they reached puberty and needed separation from SAN's teenage girls. Up to 120 young men lived at different times in the Flor Azul dormitory, attended school, worked the farm, and learned agricultural business and vocational trade skills like carpentry, tailoring, and computers. Over the course of a decade, the Flor Azul boys successfully grew papayas and tomatoes, tended goats and chickens, and farmed a tilapia pond. Many of these teenagers eventually attended the technical college in Tegucigalpa, and in addition to agriculture they studied electronics, mechanics, and engineering for manufacturing jobs.

After the farm was wired for electricity, a group from Spain built large greenhouses there to grow varieties of fruits and vegetables. Sister María Rosa made a decision in 2012 to move the SAN boys from the isolation of Flor Azul to her Nuevo Paraiso village, into a two-house compound named Santiago Apóstol. From there they can walk to high school, live in a larger community, and be reunited with younger siblings in the children's homes. Flor Azul is now used solely for farming projects.

⚜

BESIDES THESE SOCIAL PROGRAMS, SISTER MARÍA ROSA helped many of her grown children get started in careers when it was time to leave the nest. Some managed microenterprises like SAN's Leopoldina and Posada Azul guesthouses for volunteers and visitors, the Ciclos de Honduras brick factory, the Maderas carpentry shop, the Aurora Cafeteria at the clinic, the Mama Coakley dining hall at Nuevo Paraíso, the SAN bakery, the Tajiricas plantain chip factory, a jelly factory, a tailor shop, and a cement block factory, among other businesses. Others worked directly for SAN and helped manage the social projects, the office, or some of Sister María Rosa's money-making ventures, such as a mini-market in Miraflores and several agriculture and livestock projects at Flor Azul.

Sister María Rosa's conviction that her grown children should leave the project with a college degree or a trade has produced several generations of trained and educated adults who are able to support themselves and their families and contribute to the economy.

"SAN raised me, protected me, and gave me an education; Sister was like my real mother," said María Antonia Piñeda Saldivar, a beauty products business owner. She sent her own child to study electrical engineering at the National Autonomous University of Honduras.

Another grown child of SAN, Victor Manuel Sierra, became a furniture designer and teacher. "SAN gave me the opportunity to study furniture design here and also in Germany," he said. "Because of SAN I feel I am a better man and have a good profession and wonderful marriage."

In the years of reconstruction after Hurricane Mitch, while most child welfare organizations struggled to rebuild or regroup, SAN made strides toward its own sustainability by creating new programs to educate, train, heal, and transition its children into a productive adulthood. Certainly there were projects that failed or fell by the wayside. These lasting successful ones, such as the Reyes Irene Valenzuela Institute, Santa Rosa de Lima Clinic, Flor Azul Farm, and Pedro Atala Homes, reflect Sister María Rosa's absolute insistence on education, health care, meaningful work, and dignity for the poor. Sister María Rosa nurtured in her children an entrepreneurial spirit, the same spirit that prompted her to create a project in response to any need that crossed her path. Her "teach them to fish" philosophy ensured that SAN's programs and microenterprises—and its grown children—would be self-sustaining in a poor country where follow-through is countercultural.

"What I wanted to do was to start some things and then pass them over to my children to manage," Sister María Rosa said. "We did this many times. That way, when they leave Sociedad, they have a place to work. Sometimes it works well, sometimes not so well.

"If I would measure a project for money, I would have to stop right now. If I measure a project for human needs, I can never stop. I say to God, 'If You want me to do that, find a way for me to pay for it.' He has to do His part. We always work together."

PROFILE: THE CHILD OF SAN WHO WORKS WITH SISTER MARÍA ROSA'S FOUNDATION

Gerardo Enrique "Quique" Rodriguez

Gerardo Enrique "Quique" Rodriguez was 15 days old when his destitute mother placed him in Sister María Rosa's arms. He grew up as one of Sister María Rosa's sons, living first in SAN Aldeas S.O.S.'s Kennedy homes and later at its Zamoranito farm. As an adult, he internalized her teachings to found the nonprofit Global Brigades, an international student-led organization dedicated to rural community development in Honduras, Nicaragua, Panama, and Ghana. Today he runs several businesses with his wife and volunteers on the board of Sister María Rosa's personal foundation, helping raise money to fund retirement payments for SAN's aging and elderly workers.

"I think the best thing that happened in my life was to end up in

*Sister's project," said Rodriguez. "I had the best childhood. In school,
other kids could tell I was from the orphanage because of my clothes
and they would ask me, 'How come you kids from the orphanage look
happier than the kids with parents?' And I would say, 'This is my
life. I like it and I am well.'"*

*Rodriguez credits Sister María Rosa with his education not just
in school but in life.*

*"Sister taught us how to love each other," he said. "The ones who
grow up in a home together are called* hermanos de casa, *brothers
of the house. When you grow up together like that with someone
who is not a relative, there is a strong link that unites us until we
die. When I see one of these people who grew up with me, we hug
and talk and that person feels more important to me than a real
brother or sister. Sister was able to create that link for us."*

*When Rodriguez as a teenager showed great talent in singing
and playing piano, SAN arranged for him to go to Honduras's
national school of music. A couple visiting Sister María Rosa from
Mannheim, Germany, invited him to study classical piano in
Germany, but after several months he was homesick for his SAN
family. He came back to Honduras, taught music in SAN's projects,
and played in several Tegucigalpa bands. Because he was only 17, he
had to get permission to leave the SAN homes some nights to
perform.*

*At one point Sister María Rosa mentioned to him that SAN
could really use a lawyer. "She said that a lot of the time we didn't
know anything about the kids' personal histories when they came to
SAN," recalled Rodriguez. "Back then people would just throw the
kids on our doorstep, or bring kids from an accident or the hospital,
and we wouldn't have even a real name or a birth date for them." So
Rodriguez used the income from his music gigs to study international
law, graduating from the National University of Honduras. He then
studied English in Houston, Texas, for a couple of years, but again*

was homesick and returned to Honduras. Instead of becoming SAN's lawyer he found passion in working with SAN's medical brigades, so he trained as an EMT at Saint Francis Hospital in Indianapolis. This moved him directly into the health projects he would start with Global Brigades.

In 2003, he and an American partner, Duffy Casey, founded a project for North American medical student volunteers to come to Honduras to serve on rural medical brigades. They called it Global Medical Relief. "We both thought what Sister María Rosa was doing was great, and we had close relationships with some of the rural communities in Honduras," Rodriguez said. "We wanted to create something serious and effective and sustainable, bringing volunteers into Honduras to do medical care."

The first five universities involved soon grew to 10, then 30, then more than 100. Along the way, Global Medical Relief disbanded, and Rodriguez and others established Global Medical Brigades, which eventually became Global Brigades, with hundreds of university chapters in the United States, Canada, and Europe. One night, when every one of Global Brigades's housing compounds across Honduras was full of volunteers, Rodriguez counted a thousand visitors.

"We grew the business because we figured out that we needed to add preparation and follow-up for the communities we served," Rodriguez explained. "You cannot change a community by just going in every six months and giving parasite meds to the kids. You have to motivate people to maintain and sustain projects. So we added water brigades and public health programs like eco-stoves, water storage units, concrete floors. Next we started creating small community buildings, casas comunales, for people to come together and meet or celebrate. Then we created rural community banks and micro-financing to empower the community.

"This was a lesson I learned from Sister: Don't just give a fish to

a guy. We have to teach people not to expect others to give them stuff; they have to work together to build the latrine or the eco-stove."

Rodriguez dedicated himself to the work, but said he ran into differences with the growing business side of the organization.

"I brought inspiration to the project, and had the love for the people and the communities," he noted. "The business side is important and necessary, but I am always more on the Sister María Rosa/humanity side, the soul side."

In 2016, when Sister María Rosa invited him to join the board of Fundación Asistencial María Rosa, her new enterprise to support the retired employees of SAN, Rodriguez left Global Brigades and began working directly with Sister. "This foundation was not about playing with the kids or working with volunteers, but instead was to create businesses to support the elderly people who had worked with Sister for 30, 40, 50, 60 years," he said. "They gave all their youth and energy to work with her, and in Honduras we don't have programs to help people after they retire. So her foundation operates some businesses that help the poor and the profits go toward providing a little money and some food each month to those retired SAN workers."

Rodriguez called or visited Sister María Rosa weekly in her later years, sometimes bringing his young son, Leonardo, or "Quiquito." He said that work and life challenges in his forties drew him home to her.

"I always found a lot of inspiration from Sister in the day-to-day situations in my life," he said. "When I need to get back on track, I try to follow her steps. She was my source of love, a source of knowledge for anyone who wants to do something for the poor. I want to keep doing the work she was doing."

CHAPTER 10

BECOMING AN INSTITUTION

SAN GROWS FROM A GRASSROOTS MISSION INTO A PARTNERSHIP OF INTERNATIONAL NGOS

--"The world is so complicated today with too many rules and too many strategic things. It's too technical with all the numbers and plans. God is not technical. God is love, and love can never be technical. We have to forget all those lines and numbers and just keep going in God's name!"--

SAN's transformation from a grassroots response to poverty into an organized nongovernmental organization (NGO) was inevitable but not easy. Hurricane Mitch's catastrophic damage attracted mission team after mission team to SAN from the United States and Canada; the groups brought medicine, food, shoes and clothing for suffering Hondurans. In hosting the mission groups, SAN's operations ballooned—and so did the demand to codify its principles and practices, not to mention its finances, relating to all the mission volunteers and international donors.

Sister María Rosa had a very successful track record of

meeting imperative needs on a case-by-case basis. For more than three decades, she simply directed all of SAN's resources toward the urgent demand of the moment, meeting that immediate need or solving that problem. In the new century, however, the sheer numbers of desperately poor children and families were overwhelming, and SAN struggled to keep up on its own. After Hurricane Mitch, more and more of its resources began to come from abroad, from Canada and Europe and the United States, sometimes with strings attached.

Certainly these international mission teams set SAN on a path of long-term sustainability, and Sister María Rosa was grateful. Churches, medical programs, universities, and high schools sent volunteer groups to stay in SAN's guesthouses and donate money, goods, and labor. The material donations they brought—clothing, shoes, medicine, tools, water filters, toiletries, and cash—were extremely scarce in post-Mitch Honduras. Mission travelers came to work on construction and maintenance of children's homes; to donate books, backpacks, school supplies, uniforms, and desk chairs to SAN's schools; to bring down donations from large fundraisers; to conduct rural medical and dental brigades; and to write grant proposals and offer business mentoring. These people were charmed by the story of SAN and by Sister María Rosa herself. They fell in love with her children, who rushed out to play and to lead them by the hand to show them their rooms, their schoolwork, their prowess with a soccer ball.

In addition to material donations, the mission travelers brought to disaster-weary Honduras the fresh, can-do energy of noncombatants. Yet they required care and handling, room and board, bottled water and safely prepared food, comfortable transportation, translators, and explanations—

in English—of everything they were seeing. Sister María Rosa was exceptionally savvy at building relationships with the mission teams. She was honest, frank, and very direct, welcoming the visitors warmly into her project and then boldly asking if they could provide whatever SAN needed at the moment. She put SAN's key staffers in position to coordinate logistics and facilitate the mission trips. Mae Valenzuela, Sonia Erazo, Pancho Paz, Cato Elvir, and Carlos Aguilar, among others, all became liaisons for and friends with the North American groups. Most of them had spent time living and studying in the United States and spoke excellent English. Travelers felt cared for and bonded in friendship, so they made immediate plans to return.

Sister María Rosa also recognized the opportunity to solicit child sponsors from the visitors. She was convinced that more developed and economically stable First World countries could aid the Third World best by supporting its children, its future. In SAN's early days, child sponsorship came almost entirely from Hondurans, but homegrown support had waned over the years, especially after Mitch.

In 2007, SAN hired Anabellsy Vallejos Tellez, a schoolteacher from Nicaragua, as director of development, and she soon took over child sponsorship. Vallejos met with visiting mission and brigade teams to market SAN's mission, history, and successes to potential sponsors. She gave compelling descriptions of her trips with a social worker to bring children to SAN from their unlivable dwellings or unfit mothers, and then showed the visitors how well the kids were doing now. These emotional appeals in Vallejos's excellent and soft-spoken English helped expand child sponsorship tremendously among North American donors. Her responsiveness to SAN's international partners helped grow sponsorship from about 100 sponsors when she started to more than 1,000 today.

Money and expertise from abroad represented real growth for SAN, and Sister María Rosa bolstered new relationships with benefactors by engaging them intimately in her core mission and treating them like family. She warmly welcomed the groups, telling them, "It's good you should come here. This is a good school for you—not in books, but in our children. Every single child is a different world!" Then she began advocating for them to come back soon, planting the seeds of returning even before their mission week was over. She reinforced in travelers the notion that each of them was personally important and vital to her work and that they were sent to this mission by God.

"You are in this work and God is in this work. He wants you here," Sister María Rosa exhorted the mission teams. "It's not my fault—I didn't know you! But He knows you."

Thanks to Sister María Rosa's intimate welcome and insistence that the volunteer groups are part of SAN's family, a huge percentage of SAN's annual mission travelers are returnees from previous trips. In my own parish, most team members come back to Honduras for a second, third, 10th, or even 20th mission trip. These are not just the adults with financial means to buy the costly plane ticket, but young people, too: Teen travelers in my Indianapolis groups work hard to raise money for an annual trip to Honduras during their college summers. Every year, at least seventy percent of my adult team members are returnees deeply involved in sponsoring Honduran children, providing college scholarships, and supporting Friends of Honduran Children Indiana's fundraising for SAN. Other groups who come to SAN regularly from Canada and Cleveland likewise bring more return travelers than new ones. In SAN's volunteer circles it's very common to hear, "I thought I was just going on a one-week mission trip, but then I listened to Sister María Rosa and knew I was definitely coming back!"

In recent years before COVID-19, SAN hosted an average of 25 mission groups each year, varying in size from a dozen to about 80 people. Among the people who come regularly to SAN are church teams from Cleveland, Indianapolis, Seattle, and Tacoma; students from universities and medical schools throughout North America and from high schools in Ohio, Florida, and Indiana; and groups of friends, families, and coworkers from Chicago, Oshkosh, Wisconsin, and Peterborough, Ontario. Five of these long-returning groups formed not-for-profit organizations to help administer child sponsorships and international donations for SAN. Sister María Rosa called them her North American partners and family.

"In the beginning I got support from local Honduran citizens who just like me believed in a future for our children," she wrote in a letter to donors. "Now there are several organizations from the United States, Canada, and Europe who help us maintain our projects and they have my eternal gratitude. They may come in groups, in pairs or all alone, but they have one objective in mind: to share time with my children, to improve lives, or just simply to carry in their hearts the memory that they had a chance to make this a better world. I thank our Lord for the love and joy that binds us together as a big family under the same roof that stretches for thousands of kilometers."

The first and oldest partner organization, Friends of Honduran Children Canada (FOHC), was incorporated in 1993 in Peterborough, Ontario, after Jim McCallum had been coming down to help Sister Maria Rosa in Honduras for many years. Today it is a registered Canadian charity with annual operations close to a million Canadian dollars. They facilitate more than 600 child sponsorships at Nuevo Paraíso, Pedro Atala, and the Reyes Irene Valenzuela project. They bring many mission teams to Honduras for construction, medical, and education brigades, raise funds for scholarships for SAN's deserving students, and offer a microloan program for young women at the Reyes Irene Valenzuela Institute who want to start their own businesses.

Friends of Honduran Children (FHC) Indiana was incorporated in Indianapolis, Indiana, in 2001 by members of the first mission group that Father Jeff Godecker brought down from Immaculate Heart of Mary Church. Its mission is to support the health, education, and welfare of the children of Honduras and to promote Honduran self-sufficiency. Besides the administration of hundreds of child sponsorships, FHC Indiana members have overseen the funding of university scholarships and the new medical clinic of a grown child of SAN, business planning and operations for a brick factory and a computer education center, the development of marketing and grant materials for SAN, a study of pediatric asthma in rural Honduras, and several mission trips a year. They are especially focused on education, including "transition" housing and programs to help SAN's high school graduates move on to university or trade school or a job and learn independent living skills. (Disclosure: I have been a member of FHC Indiana's board of directors since 2008.)

Honduran Children's Rescue Fund (HCRF) was founded in 2004 by a group of frequent mission travelers from Church of the Gesu in University Heights, Ohio, near Cleveland, led on their first trip by Father Lorn Snow, S.J. The organization leads medical brigades, raises money through benefits, grants, and donations, and is especially dedicated to SAN's Reyes Irene Valenzuela Institute and the Santa Rosa de Lima Clinic. HCRF transports large medical equipment down to Honduras via military cargo planes and pays the salary of the sole doctor staffing the clinic since the 2009 coup. Members of HCRF were instrumental in helping upgrade Santa Rosa de Lima Clinic into a Regional Medical Facility in Honduras.

Hope for Honduran Children (H4HC) was formed in Shaker Heights, Ohio, in 2004 by John and Karen Godt. They formed a special relationship with the teenage boys of SAN's Flor Azul Youth Farm. H4HC led mission brigades, built an internet cafe and gift shop/convenience store at Nuevo Paraíso, instituted training programs in handicrafts, carpentry, and other trades, and oversaw several farming ventures at Flor Azul. No longer affiliated with SAN, H4HC today runs a program called Casa Noble that facilitates sponsorships and scholarships for some of the older teen boys who used to live at Flor Azul. They opened two homes in the village of Santa Lucía to house dozens of young men— some former SAN kids and some from rural mountain communities—now studying in high schools and universities in the capital.

Virtù, Inc, was established in 2008 by David Bower, formerly of FHC Indiana, to support education initiatives for children at SAN's Pedro Atala Homes. Virtù provides scholarships to private high schools for academically eligible students, employs an English teacher and tutor to help with homework, and recently opened two houses adjacent to the Pedro Atala Homes for young women transitioning out of SAN and into trade or university education in Tegucigalpa.

Its mission groups provide Pedro Atala children with Christmas gifts, renovations, new construction in their compound, and other support.

Several of these groups have joined together on larger projects or emergency needs: child sponsorship, renovating bathrooms at Pedro Atala, building a security wall around Nuevo Paraíso, updating the clinic, providing a new roof for the Reyes Irene Valenzuela school, shortfall funding for Flor Azul, and other challenges. Sister María Rosa knew that these partnerships would sustain SAN by leveraging relationships and resources outside Honduras.

"The North American groups are *excelente*," she said. "If we would not have them here we couldn't keep going. They come not only to give the money but to train my people. This is good. We appreciate it very much."

With North American involvement, however, came North American business methodologies and strong opinions about how SAN should operate its programs and allocate its funds. The partner organizations urged SAN to develop and follow a business strategy to ensure its sustainability. They recommended that SAN create a website and publications, grow child sponsorship, establish an endowment, expand the volunteer visitor program, attract new donors, and demand more support from the Honduran government, which had been spotty at best. Successive SAN strategic plans, painstakingly crafted with the initial help of Peter White and David Cain from FOHC and Jack Licate of HCRF, are meant to be checked against a scorecard of long-term objectives, in order to help SAN's management team see beyond the day-to-day emergencies to implement long-term guidelines, priorities, and sustainable business practices. The North Americans want their donations to be investments in the future of SAN.

"SAN's sustainability became a bigger issue only in recent years," said Phyllis Stewart-Hope of FHC Indiana. "Really, for the first several times we went down there, the most obvious things we saw were displacement and extreme poverty. It was a time of recovery and just meeting the immediate needs of the people. Today, of course, it isn't a hand-to-mouth situation anymore, as when Sister started SAN. It's one thing to directly shelter, feed, clothe, and educate kids. But it's much more complex when you have to account for large international donations and sponsorships for children."

In terms of sustainability, it is difficult for the visionary to run things effectively over the long haul.

"An institution cannot stand totally on the charism of its founder—it's always messy, never ideal," said Father Jeff Godecker, who led the first mission trips to SAN from his Indianapolis parish of Immaculate Heart of Mary. "As with many if not most spiritual movements, the charisms of the founder attract a great following, which then demands organization, growth, and institutionalization in order to continue. Saint Francis, for example, led this freewheeling life, but then his men got organized into the Franciscans. Likewise, there was the man Jesus and then the organizing of Christianity."

So Sister María Rosa faced the same dilemma as the founder of her religious order, Saint Francis: How can you control or even slow the ardent momentum of your own movement? Saint Francis and Sister María Rosa both wanted to steer clear of any kind of methodization; both desired to serve the needs of the poor in an unsystematic way, from among them. Against Saint Francis's wishes, his brother monks eventually strained toward standardization, permanent housing, and papal approval; for Sister María Rosa, a larger operation of her projects demanded policies and detailed accounting.

There are other parallels between these two visionaries, as well. Just as Saint Francis left his rich merchant father to serve the destitute, Sister María Rosa left behind the relative comfort and familiarity of La Policlínica and her community of Sisters to live with destitute children. And as Saint Francis increasingly disowned his family's wealth, burrowing more deeply into place with the outcasts and the hermits, Sister María Rosa rejected comfort when she split from the financial security of S.O.S. Kinderdorf to follow her own vision.

Standardization of practices and finances was not central to Sister María Rosa's vision, nor to the vision of Saint Francis. G. K. Chesterton in his book *Saint Francis* describes a man "who cannot see the woods for the trees," whose vision considered each tree "as a separate and almost sacred thing, being a child of God and therefore a brother or sister of man." Sister María Rosa, too, sometimes couldn't see the forest for the trees at SAN; she tilted at the individual need that rose highest or most acutely in front of her. Her campaign against poverty and the unjust treatment of women and children was never systematic or methodical. Instead, her priorities were immediate, crisis-driven, and right in front of her face: She needed to find a house for Marta and her six children, safety from the gangs for the homeless boy on the bridge, a special-needs school for Carlos, groceries for Gabriela, medicine for the baby.

In Sister María Rosa's view, "comprehensive" or "systematic" acts were not what the Lord required of her. He asked her to help Marta, Carlos, Gabriela—right this minute. And she would not say no because SAN or its supporting organizations had adopted guidelines against something she felt called to do. She would never say no to the Lord because her houses were full or there was no money. Instead, she believed that the Lord would always provide. Period.

"I used to be able to just take in the street kids, but now, if I find a little child and bring him to a home, they say it is against the law," Sister María Rosa said. "Now you cannot do the good things because all the people question it. I pray every moment: 'Lord, please help me. I want to be free to help the poor, not to have someone say yes, you can help this person but no, you cannot help that child.'"

As with any multinational partnerships, cultural misunderstandings between Sister María Rosa and the North Americans were bound to occur, with best intentions sometimes lost in translation. Overall, everyone's goal to help the children was in lockstep. There were days, however, when the North Americans didn't grasp the direct and immediate way Sister María Rosa approached the urgent needs of the poor, times when they could not fathom why she might spend donations on questionable ventures with financial risk. Likewise, there were times when Sister María Rosa had little patience with the directive from the North Americans that SAN first draw up a plan with estimates before it could have the money that each organization had raised.

"To me, it is very hard to hear from the North Americans that I shouldn't be working like I do, that I have to have a strategic plan for everything," Sister María Rosa told me. "Sometimes they want to put me in a square box and say, 'You must do it this way; otherwise you cannot get our help.' I tell them, 'Why do we need that? We have the Ten

Commandments, and we have the Lord's law to love one another as He has loved us. He didn't give us these laws any other way. You will mix me up with these plans. I have been listening to the Lord since I was six years old and what He wants me to do is not numbers, but to answer the knock at the door and give the people what they need. The needs of the people are always there, bigger and bigger.

"Why did the Lord feed so many people in the mountains with the loaves and fishes? If that had to be part of a strategic plan, those people would never be fed!'"

Exasperated when told what to do by outsiders, Sister María Rosa often declared: "God save us from rich people and *politicos*!"

To illustrate that point, Mae Valenzuela once told a story of a very rich North American man who came to check out SAN and donate to the organization. Sister María Rosa sent Valenzuela with him to see the Nuevo Paraíso project, where he was dismayed by the number of abandoned children needing homes.

"He asked me, 'Why do all these Honduran women keep getting pregnant and have all these kids that end up here?'" Valenzuela remembered. "Actually, he used much cruder words referring to animals. Then he said, 'If I give Sister María Rosa a million dollars would she sterilize these women?' I was shocked and told him, 'No, never! We are Catholic!' But he didn't understand at all. I was praying that he would forget his awful idea, but during breakfast with Sister, he said, 'I have the check written right here in my pocket and will give SAN a million dollars on the condition that you use it to sterilize women.' Sister actually stood up and left the table, announcing, 'I have to go. I hope you had a good stay, and enjoy your meal. Mae will take you to the airport afterward.' She walked to the door and then she turned and told him, 'You have just offended me, you have offended my country, and you have offended God. Goodbye!'"

In 2009 SAN leaders, representatives from several partner NGOs, and other non-Honduran advisors and friends of Sister María Rosa set up a SAN Advisory Board to facilitate better communication about SAN's needs and less duplication of efforts among all. They learned from one another that partnering with SAN sometimes requires the business-minded to shut off or at least mute their internal alarm systems and remember that Honduras—and Sister María Rosa in particular—does not operate like the United States or Canada.

"I think when Sister prays, God picks up the phone and calls us to come and help," wrote Michael Murphy, a Tacoma contractor and volunteer, in a flurry of emails concerning water problems at Flor Azul. "And the answer to the prayer is not to abandon our business training and experience when we see problems, but rather to share and highlight potential conflicts for SAN."

"Sister just always had the strongest will," Jack Licate of HCRF summed it up. "She told me once, 'When I need money, I pray to the Holy Spirit and it appears.' I said, 'The Holy Spirit doesn't write proposals and apply for foundation grants.' And she said, 'No, but the Holy Spirit sent me you!'

"So it's like dealing with an entrepreneur on a mission, who is going to get that mission done come hell or high water and is going to do it her way," Licate continued. "The way she knew was tried and true for her for 50 years in that environment, even with the slipperiness of funding, the inefficiency, and the corruption. She had to live in that and over-come those difficulties in helping these children."

Her partner NGOs can (and do) worry among themselves whether SAN will ever operate in the black or establish an endowment, but that was never Sister María Rosa's concern. She handled crisis management her way for more than 50 years. Rooted in an uncorrupted reliance on the Lord, her sustainability plan came from her entrenched certainty that God would always provide. So even if her tried-and-true approach to the problems in her own country bumped up against the international NGOs' need to steward their donors' money, the sponsors still sent donations and the groups still enthusiastically came down to Honduras.

"SAN is and always has been under-financed," noted Daniel Meehan, the Milwaukee philanthropist who built the Santa Rosa de Lima Clinic and served on the SAN Advisory Board. "With Sister at the helm, from the goodness of her heart accepting destitute children without a moment's concern for the bottom line—this has always been consistent with her heart full of love. SAN has accomplished more in Honduras than we have the ability to imagine, even if their financial challenges have sometimes been met by borrowing from Peter to pay Paul. Still, who in their right mind would not have been inspired to follow Sister anyway?"

Sister María Rosa with a mission team from Indianapolis

Sister María Rosa with some of Friends of Honduran
Children Indiana's SAN scholarship students

Sister María Rosa with college-age returnees on their
second trip to Honduras

PROFILE: THE TEACHER WHO GAVE UP HER CLASSROOM TO BUILD A CHILD SPONSORSHIP PROGRAM

Anabellsy Vallejos Tellez

Anabellsy Vallejos Tellez was so attracted to Sister María Rosa's mission and reputation that she left a very good position as a popular English teacher in Yoro, Honduras, to work for SAN. One month into the job, she had a better sense of its emotional magnitude and SAN's lack of resources. She wanted to resign.

"*I never imagined that working at SAN would be so hard,*" she explained. "*I came with big ideas, everything I wanted to do for the welfare of the children. I thought it would be easy to make things happen, but it wasn't. I think it's only because of God—and Sister María Rosa—that I stayed.*"

The switch from teaching to social work was not a stretch for Vallejos: She and all of her siblings chose careers in community service of some kind. They are products of hardworking parents, but also of a tragedy during their childhood in Chinandega, Nicaragua. When Vallejos was nine, during the war in Nicaragua, the Sandinistas were in power and demanded that her father, a businessman, to cooperate with them. He refused.

"*So the Sandinistas told him, 'If you are not with us you are against us,'*" Vallejos recalled. "*In 1983 my father disappeared on his way to work. His body was never found. My mother spent a year looking for him, getting lots of phone calls to go check on a dead body pulled from the sea or a body found burned in the sugarcane fields.*" (Ten years later, according to Vallejos, one of his captors confessed that the Sandinistas had killed him and thrown his body off a cliff.)

The family lost everything. Vallejos's mother, Rosa, could never collect her husband's life insurance without a death certificate and a body. Friends and neighbors avoided them for fear of the Sandinistas. The family received bomb threats warning them to stop looking for their father.

After a year, doctors told Vallejos's mother that she should move the family away for their health; young Ana had to take pills just to sleep at night. So Rosa got passports for her four children and they fled Nicaragua for Honduras—close enough to return in case of news of their husband and father. They left by taxi at 2 a.m. with one suitcase of clothing.

"*We couldn't tell anyone ahead of time that we were leaving Nicaragua,*" Vallejos said. "*As long as neighbors saw the cars still there in the morning, they wouldn't suspect we were gone. When we kids were sad about our leaving our home and all our possessions, our mother reminded us, 'I am saving the most important thing: you.'"*

In Tegucigalpa, they rented a house and bought mattresses to sleep on. Trained as an accountant, Rosa instead cleaned houses and washed clothes until she found a cashier's job. She soon added a second job in a factory. In time she earned enough money to send all her children to university.

"Watching my mother work like that gave me a lot of strength," said Vallejos. "All my siblings and I were formed into reaching and working for things we wanted instead of just thinking and dreaming about them. For each of us, if we have to take a broom and sweep, we do it. So I think God had a purpose in all that happened to our family. If we had grown up with everything, we wouldn't think of other people's needs and I might not be working with children today. I understand now that all that happened was God preparing us for His mission."

As adults, Vallejos's family was familiar with the work and mission of SAN. One brother-in-law had grown up in a SAN Aldeas S.O.S. home in Choloma, Honduras, and two brothers worked for Global Brigades in Honduras with Quique Rodriguez, one of Sister María Rosa's grown children.

"One day my brother told me that if I wanted to join Sister María Rosa's organization, this was the time to do it because there was a job open," Vallejos recalled. "I saw this as my chance. It was hard to leave my work as a teacher, though. I loved being with children in a classroom every day, teaching English, dancing and singing with them."

When she got the job in 2007, Vallejos moved with her husband, their two children, and her mother from the city of Yoro to Tegucigalpa. She came to start SAN's new development department, but soon took over sponsorship in addition. Vallejos was eager to over-

haul the sponsorship program, but was given no computer, no phone, no office (just the dining room), and no budget for mailings or for printing brochures.

"After less than two weeks, I was trying to resign, I was trying to run away," Vallejos said. "But Sister stopped me. I came in here flying and she made me land. She told me the opposite of what I expected—not the opposite of my ideas, but the way I would accomplish them. She told me, 'If you believe in God, you will handle this challenge.' And I just stayed. I still couldn't understand how she could have these workers at SAN without the tools to do their jobs. But that was the purpose of God's training since my childhood and the beginning of my road to putting faith in action—to start with ideas, but nothing in my hands, just trying to do the best I could. After a while people in the North American groups came to know me, and God touched some of those people to provide me with tools to help our program."

In her seven years at SAN before she departed to start her own service organization in Panama with family members, Vallejos grew SAN's child sponsorship program from dozens into many hundreds of sponsors. She created marketing materials for visiting groups and developed strong professional relationships with the North American NGOs. Her excellent command of English helped her convey to visitors the emotion of both the children's dire needs and their success stories.

"I will never understand what stopped me from leaving in those first weeks," she said. "I could easily have gone back to teaching school; for two years the principal kept calling to ask me to come back. I think God's hands were over me, maintaining me, keeping me at SAN. I know God's been with me in this work because many times when I had a big problem and couldn't sleep, I would wake up with the solution, sent from God.

"It's surprising, but I can see now that God called me and then

Sister María Rosa encouraged me to stay at SAN. Sister would remind me that Jesus said, 'Whoever receives one of these little children in my name receives me; and whoever receives me receives not me, but Him who sent me' (Mark 19:37). So this is how I came to fulfill my own mission to help children everywhere I go."

PROFILE: THE CONSTRUCTION MANAGER WHO LEARNED EFFICIENCY FROM THE HONDURANS

Brian Smith

The director of construction for the Cleveland Clinic believes there is a lot to be learned from watching how Hondurans build a wall or dig a hole.

"They always find the easiest way to swing an ax or shovel," Brian Smith explained. "When we bring North Americans down to Honduras, they often take the approach of go-go-go and push-push-push to get the work done as quickly as possible. I tell them to put it in check and watch how it's done here. The Hondurans are always so efficient."

This also goes for Sister Rosa, as he calls her.

"She had the same technique," he explained. "She was an entrepreneur, a capitalist. She was very efficient at getting things done because she always found the shortest distance between two points. She found the easiest way. If she was given a gift of anything, within minutes or hours it ended up in the hands of someone else who needed it. She could build a hospital or a program without any money—things like that. I know it was a point of frustration for people who wanted audits and ledgers and plans. And it got the organization into a fair amount of fiscal trouble with utility bills, severance payments, and taxes not being paid. But she had only one goal—to directly help those in need. I have to think there's nothing she wouldn't try to make a go of."

Smith said he was always struck by another form of Sister María Rosa's efficiency: When she brought her hands together to pray, her wrists made a perfect 90-degree angle so that her fingers pointed straight up to God.

"Her prayer position was always so natural, with no straining," he remarked. "Which is good, since she spent so much time in prayer and adoration—two and a half hours every morning before breakfast!"

Smith, 59, first came to Honduras after Hurricane Mitch to lead building brigades for his pastor, Father Lorn Snow of Church of the Gesu outside Cleveland. Smith says the Hondurans let him know that they could do the construction themselves; they only needed money for the materials. The greater necessity was health care. So the Gesu group began to support SAN's Santa Rosa de Lima Clinic by paying a staff doctor's salary, shipping medical equipment, and helping with maintenance, repairs, and additions. In 2004 the group founded Honduran Children's Rescue Fund to help SAN with not only the clinic but also the Reyes Irene Institute. Brian's father, David Smith, was the first president, and Brian recently took over the top position. "We formed the organization because we knew we wanted to raise money, in addition to exposing people to SAN through mission trips," David Smith said.

Brian Smith never expected to find himself so often in Honduras:

more than 60 times since that first mission trip. "I did not even know what the word hola *(hello) meant," he said. "I had no idea where Honduras was. I was driving home from work and heard a story on NPR about Hurricane Mitch from a city with a strange-sounding name: Tegucigalpa. Since that first trip, I've drawn a line between Cleveland and Tegucigalpa and realized I've never been any place in between the two cities."*

All of Smith's children have traveled to Honduras. When his daughter wrote in her medical school application that her Honduras experience prompted her career choice, Smith told her he had no idea Honduras was that meaningful to her.

"You just don't realize the effect Honduras has on people," he said. "For me the opportunity to come here was life-changing. It's such a privilege to be with people during the most intimate times in their lives: family deaths, life events, even climbing out of poverty."

Both David and Brian Smith had heard and read about Sister María Rosa before they met her. "I knew a lot about her even before my first trip," Brian Smith recalled. "I had heard she was called the Mother Teresa of Honduras. In that day, her picture was hanging in the Tegucigalpa airport. Whenever we would stop at a military roadblock, one of the first things out of my mouth, in broken Spanish, was 'I am working with Sister María Rosa and Sociedad Amigos de los Niños.' And then the guards with the guns would smile and one of them would say, 'Oh, that's my mother!'"

After decades of traveling down to Honduras, Smith thinks of Sister María Rosa as a matriarch who formed and led soldiers. "Our battle is against poverty," he said. "We've always taken comfort in the fact that as long as we were aligned with Sister Rosa, we were doing the right thing. Even if something did not make a ton of sense at the moment.

"She had the purity of a young lady making her First Communion. The rest of the world starts out young and idealistic, too, but

loses that as they experience hardships and the realities of life and allow all that to take root. There were times in Honduras where her life was threatened and she had to travel with guards; I would challenge anyone not to become jaded by that. Instead, she was still that little girl who was taught by the nuns. She had tremendous faith that she and God were very much aligned and that the work she was doing was really God's work. So she just kept going and did what needed to be done."

Apart from his family and children, Smith believes that Sister María Rosa was the factor that most drew him outside of himself.

"She was my role model, and I make no secret about the fact that I'm in this for life," he said. "Like she did, I will just keep going. It's like that line from the movie As Good As It Gets: *She made us all want to be better people."*

CHAPTER 11

LETTING GO

SISTER MARÍA ROSA TURNS SAN LEADERSHIP OVER TO OTHERS… SORT OF

~~"God pays very well. He is the best one to work for."~~

SAN celebrated its 50th anniversary in March 2016 to much fanfare in the Honduran media. *La Prensa* newspaper praised Sister María Rosa as "a humanitarian institution in Honduras," extolling her "deep sensitivity and love for others, possessed of an unyielding and tenacious faith in her mission of giving shelter to the disadvantaged, especially orphans and children at social risk." Another newspaper, *La Tribuna*, described SAN as a "worthy institution founded by a noble religious nun who was humbled by orphanhood and who nestled in her soul an endearing love for homeless children." This article congratulated SAN on founding homes designed not to isolate children from the world but to integrate them into society in "colonies" where they could go to school and be trained to become men and women useful to the country. It named many Tegucigalpans who supported Sister María Rosa and SAN: the doctors with whom she worked at La Policlínica (Enrique Aguilar, Salvador Paredes, Adá Zepeda, Manuel Bueso, Silvio and César Zúniga); businessmen who helped found SAN (Salomón Kafati, Eduardo Kawas, José Rafael Ferrari, Pedro Atala, Óscar Kafati, Manuel Villeda Toledo, and Nicolás Atala); and "great women who gave assistance" (Reyes Valenzuela, Regina Vargas de Aguilar, Celina León Gómez de Urrutia, Ana Lourdes Zúñiga de Paredes, Myrna Díaz de Mejía, and Carolina Agüero de Agurcia).

Hondurans in very high positions testified their support and admiration for Sister María Rosa's work as well. Aguas Ocaña Navarro, Honduras's First Lady from 2003 to 2006, declared Sister María Rosa to be "an extraordinary person who has devoted her life to the betterment, care and education of thousands of children and young people in our country.... Her labor of love... has won the affection and respect of her people and the international community." Roberto Micheletti Bain, then president of the National Congress, said, "We thank Sor María Rosa for saving so many lives and we feel proud to have our own Honduran 'Mother Teresa.'" Cardinal Rodríguez wrote that he was "pleased to give my support and full endorsement to the programs of Sociedad Amigos de los Niños...[which has provided] food and housing, education and health care, thus giving children an opportunity to forge their own productive futures in the light of God's will."

SAN's 50th birthday celebration represented a special recognition of Sister María Rosa's body of work in Honduras, but it was just the tip of the iceberg of all the awards that came during Sister María Rosa's eighth and ninth decades.

In 1997, Sister María Rosa won Favorite Daughter status from her hometown municipality of Puerto Cortés, followed in 1998 by a gold medal from the municipal corporation of the central district of Honduras. Also in 1998 she became the first woman to receive the Tegucigalpa Chamber of Commerce and Industry's Gold Leaf award, a "spirit of service" prize normally reserved for Honduran men. In 1999 the School Sisters of Saint Francis recognized her for 50 years of service to the poor, and she also won Tegucigalpa's Laura Vigil de Lozano International Woman of the Year award. From Rotary International in 2004 she received the Paul Harris prize. In 2007 Casa Alianza gave Sister María Rosa an award for "invaluable work, love, solidarity and dedication to the disfavored and excluded men and women of Honduras." In 2008 she was featured for the second time on a Honduran postage stamp.

In June 2009 she traveled to Milwaukee to receive an honorary degree from Marquette University, which over the preceding decade had sent more than 200 students, professors, and staff to volunteer with SAN. Associate senior vice president Doctor Thomas J. (Toby) Peters introduced her as "a humble servant of God who over the past 50 years has raised and educated more than 40,000 Honduran orphans." Then Sister María Rosa received a doctorate of humane letters, *honoris causa,* for her "extraordinary acts of compassion, for being an inspiration to people all over the world, and for exemplifying the spirit of *magis* by being a woman for others." She stood onstage grinning brightly, looking short and small but very powerful in black graduation robes, white hood, and blue-and-white sash, as she received a very rare standing ovation from the packed stadium.

In April 2011 she received an award from the Martin

Luther King Jr. Foundation for her "labor for the most poor and needy of society." In 2014, the Honduran Ministry of Education declared Sister María Rosa one of six national heroes whose lives will be studied by children in Honduran grade schools. A year later she was named an "exemplary citizen" by a retirees' association of the National Autonomous University of Honduras. Sister María Rosa was included in a 2015 list of distinguished women by the Central American Parliament in Guatemala City. The mayor of Indianapolis, Indiana, named March 5, 2016, as Sister María Rosa Day to honor her work and affiliation with FHC Indiana. Later in 2016, Honduras's national anticorruption agency awarded Sister María Rosa a five-star distinction for "integrity and transparency" in her work for Honduran citizens.

In 2016 she received tribute from Honduras's National Congress for her 50-year labor for the country, and an emotional recognition on Honduras's Children's Day from Dirección de Niñez, Adolescencia y Familia (DINAF), the country's child and family services agency, for being an exemplary orphan. El Banco Central de Honduras in 2016 named Sister María Rosa a model of justice, equality, and solidarity in Honduras. On a national holiday in 2018 she received recognition as an exemplary citizen from another Honduran bank, and in 2020 she won the first award for Women of Peace and Security from the Honduran secretary of security through the office of the vice minister of prevention and the national police.

More than 50 years after Sister María Rosa started SAN with no funding at all, the organization's annual operations budget now totals $2.5 million. SAN does receive financial support from the Honduran government—a commitment that has grown in recent years since DINAF stopped operating residential homes of its own. Today it refers at-risk children to organizations like SAN and provides about 5,000 lempiras (around $200) annually per child. The government also pays some salaries at SAN. The support is unpredictable and inconsistent, however: Often the funds come very late or not at all. In 2017 DINAF's first disbursement of funds to SAN for the year did not arrive until May.

"Although government support has increased recently, it is very uncertain and will differ every year," noted SAN's administrator, Alejandra Lorenzana. "The government can modify its funding without warning if it wants to."

Working more closely with the Honduran government has its benefits, but also its challenges. There have been times when SAN was overwhelmed by the large number of children referred to them by the government. I happened to be at Nuevo Paraíso in July 2015 when a whopping 15 new babies arrived within a few short months. Several of Nuevo Paraíso's 12 children's homes were suddenly populated with not one, but two children younger than 18 months. In addition, some of the babies came with significant physical or developmental difficulties. This put a tremendous strain on resources like formula, diapers, and the housemothers' time and attention. Two concerned young visitors, recent graduates of Cleveland's Gilmour Academy on a mission trip to SAN, posted an online CrowdRise campaign called $15 for 15 Babies and quickly raised $31,000 to help SAN support all the new children.

Foreign aid—some of it from crisis-driven fundraisers like that CrowdRise campaign—makes up the larger part of SAN's operations budget. This aid comes in the form of child sponsorships and scholarships, project money for new construction or maintenance, and funding for whatever is needed, provided by partner NGOs, international mission groups, and private benefactors. While she was grateful for the support from outside Honduras, this was not the model Sister María Rosa wanted. As a Honduran who grew up in a town that saw boom and then abandonment by the banana industry, Sister María Rosa often said that North American involvement in and support of SAN is not a forever guarantee. "We still fight for the government and people in our country to recognize that Hondurans should be helping Hondurans," she sighed in frustration.

In its current strategic plan, SAN wants to strengthen its fundraising (especially at home in Honduras), develop new projects, improve its marketing and communication, and implement plans to give individual and specialized attention to each child. This last goal is an urgent priority as large classes of SAN kids are graduating high school and preparing to embark on self-sufficient adult lives. There is no cookie-cutter approach for sending all of these young adults out into the world: Some are able to pass university entrance exams, some decide to enroll in vocational training or the military, and others need help finding a job, any job. Sister María Rosa knew that without help, without some program of transition, some of SAN's kids could wind up pregnant too young, inducted into gangs, flunking out of university, or moving back home with the abusive or impoverished family from which they were rescued. Children raised in SAN's safety and shelter, especially those living in rural Nuevo Paraíso, still need to learn life skills like managing a budget or bank account, navigating public transportation, maintaining an apartment, and managing study or work time.

SAN's first Transition home, Casa Santa María (Holy Mary House), was built adjacent to the Pedro Atala Homes in Tegucigalpa in 2015 by Virtú, Inc., for six young women going to university or other schools. The girls receive a monthly stipend and coaching to help them manage their own affairs; they share responsibility for the house, groceries, and cleaning. To accommodate a large bubble of high school graduates moving from Nuevo Paraiso to study at university and trade schools in Tegucigalpa, the two Friends of Honduran Children organizations in Indiana and Canada rented a second house for women, named Dios en Casa (God in the House), and the first one for boys, named Sor María Rosa Casa (Sister María Rosa House). Soon after, Virtú, Inc constructed a second Casa Santa María house for girls at Pedro Atala. In early 2020, close to 30 young adults were supported in SAN's Transition program, mostly in these houses, with a few residing in the homes of SAN staffers or in rooms and apartments on their own.

"Opening Transition homes has been quite a learning process," said Carolina Agüero de Agurcia, SAN's board president, who worked as Sister María Rosa's administrative assistant from 1981 to 1992, returning to SAN in 2014 after a career in banking. "We have had lots of great results but also a few setbacks with some students. In our newest strategic plan, we are looking at creating a pre-Transition program to further prepare SAN kids to live successfully on their own."

Most child rescue organizations cut kids off at the age of 18, so the Transition program is unusual and forward-thinking. Legally, SAN is guardian to its children only until age 18, but Sister María Rosa resolved to support the kids who go to university or into training programs until they are finished. This follow-through might be Sister María Rosa's greatest legacy: She always held that young people were not ready to strike out on their own at 18 or 20. ("They are not good people yet," she often said.) She had been adept at finding them additional job training and grounding in life skills ever since the 1970s and '80s, when she expanded her reach beyond her partnership with S.O.S. Kinderdorf to create group homes for these older kids.

"Young people need to be helped all the way through their schooling," she reiterated firmly. "Now you can find my grown children all over this country and anyplace in the world. The first one from Sociedad who became a doctor was a child we found in the public market searching the garbage for something to eat. He hadn't eaten for three days when he came to us. He studied well in school and was sponsored to go to Switzerland to become a doctor. Now he has a good practice and a family there.

"I have doctors, engineers, bookkeepers, teachers, all kinds," she continued proudly. "For each child who started here I just prayed to God, 'Give me the knowledge to help this child. Give me the way that I can make this boy or girl the way You would want them to be.'"

⚜

IN THE LAST DECADE SAN BEGAN WORKING ON ANOTHER kind of transition, too.

Even before the organization turned 50 and Sister María Rosa turned 90, questions about the future loomed like an elephant in the room: What would happen to Sister María Rosa when she eventually needed to transition herself out of the leadership of her organization? How could someone so intensely focused since the age of six on helping orphans pass that vocation on to the care and keeping of others? Was SAN's existence dependent on Sister María Rosa, or could it stand alone without her laser vision and canny intuition, without her finger on the pulse of the acute needs of the poor, without her serial entrepreneurship in starting new programs and businesses, without her charisma to attract donations, sponsorship, and mission teams?

"What should they do when I die?" Sister María Rosa quipped. "Bury me, or I will smell!" She laughed and added, "Only the Lord knows when I will go. I'm not attached to anything in this world. I love the children, but I can go."

Sister María Rosa's intent to "let go," however, contradicted lifelong habits and behavior and the fact that she had executed nearly every SAN decision since 1966. She had always been at the helm of her own ship, through the hardships and hurricanes, Father Willie's murder, the breakup with S.O.S. Kinderdorf, the 2009 coup, and all the shortfalls in funding. None of it had shaken her resolve to help poor children and mothers live with dignity.

"She knew her health was diminishing, but it was very hard for her to let go of control," said Brenner, Sister María Rosa's friend in the School Sisters of Saint Francis. Brenner visited Sister María Rosa in Honduras when she sensed her friend could use a bit of companionship during a time of imminent decision-making. In Milwaukee, SAN benefactor Daniel Meehan had asked Brenner if the School Sisters could send someone to lead SAN after Sister María Rosa. Brenner responded that SAN leadership should go to the people in Honduras. This was never a sponsored institution of the religious order, she told him. It was the dream and achievement of Sister María Rosa and her Honduran staff.

"I asked María Rosa whether she thought there was a person in the organization who could take over for her," said Brenner. "She told me, 'God has a plan.' But if she waited until she was sick, it might be too late to teach her people everything she knew, to mentor her successors. So I told her, 'You might not be a voice in the future. But you are a voice right now.'"

Shortly after that conversation between Sister Maria Rosa and her friend, SAN took its first succession-planning step by announcing a new management structure:

> *Under the guidance and counsel of Sor María Rosa, an Executive Committee (EC) has been established with responsibility for managing all aspects of the organization.... This historic transition to the new team will be a significant challenge. Sor's years of wisdom and knowledge will take time to be fully learned and put into action by the EC. With the cooperation and support of all staff and our generous donors, we are confident that the EC will be successful in this mission of love and redemption.*

The EC—including SAN's administrators, project directors, and sometimes SAN's social worker or psychologist— met regularly to share expertise on SAN matters and decisions. Many of the members were raised by Sister María Rosa or by mothers who worked with her in the early days. Most had spent their lives growing up in and working for SAN projects.

"For a long time, Sister told us, 'Someone will come. God will send someone to take over SAN when it is time,'" one EC member said. "But like a mother she prepared her own children to lead; they knew her way. So like any mother, Sister would have to let her children go and take action by themselves and feel confident that what she had taught them, they would do."

"I pass on to them what little wisdom I have," Sister

María Rosa said of the EC. "Mostly I have crazy ways! And they don't feel so strong to do it the way I do it. Sometimes I have to give them a lot to think about and then come back later to see what they are thinking now. Still, I understand them; they are my children."

So the leadership of SAN will remain homegrown.

"I don't think at Sociedad you could just pay someone to do the work," Sister María Rosa said. "Some people are too high-minded to work with children or to do things for the poor. But the EC understands the needs because they live here."

To her North American partners, Sister María Rosa wrote, "I do feel fortunate to have a team that feels it is their duty and capability to take on the reins of SAN. I have let them know that I am ready to step down and continue my life in prayer and devotion, and I have asked them if they feel capable of taking over this labor of love. I can see a new brightness in their eyes and they speak with more conviction, a conviction that for the majority of them comes from the experience of having been raised under my care, of knowing what the children's needs are from having been one of them."

This new arrangement was marked by growing pains, of course. Sometimes members of the EC took Sister María Rosa's suggestions as orders and felt that she didn't trust them to do their jobs in their own way. Sometimes Sister María Rosa played the age card and accused the EC of disrespecting an old woman. Sometimes they disagreed over the usefulness of SAN's strategic plan, which Sister María Rosa argued was not necessary since the *real* plan was in her heart —God's plan. The EC sometimes bickered among themselves like the siblings they practically are. With some time, though, the team members discovered each other's strengths and learned the details, benefits, and challenges of SAN projects besides their own.

SAN's board of directors, including some very wealthy and influential children of SAN's original 1966 board, around the same time increased their involvement and support. Led by Fernando Aragón Chamorro and later Carolina Agüero de Agurcia, the board hired an executive director from outside SAN to work with the EC on solutions to ensure SAN's future. In response to a comprehensive financial audit of SAN's books, they worked on government loan forgiveness and a rightsizing of the payroll. They found, unsurprisingly, even years after the EC was formed, that Sister María Rosa was very much still in control, especially of the purse strings. No one wanted to tell her that she could not take funding designated for SAN's children and use it to address other urgent needs gnawing at her heart.

"It is not easy when somebody comes in with money and says it must be used for this and not for that," Sister María Rosa complained. "Many people come one week a year and tell us what to do, but we are the ones who are here with the problems all year."

To resolve these dilemmas, financial auditors recommended separating SAN's social programs from Sister María Rosa's money-generating or productive enterprises. So in 2015, Sister María Rosa started a new foundation, legally registered by the Public Ministry of Honduras as Fundación Asistencial María Rosa (the María Rosa Assistance Foundation). This new entity "provides humanitarian assistance to the poor and needy of Honduras" with a special emphasis on "improving the living conditions of former workers of Sociedad Amigos de los Niños that do not have a retirement that allows them to subsist in their old age." The Foundation retains a board of directors separate from SAN's, though some members are former SAN employees. "I want my foundation to help my old employees in their retirement when they become sick or need help," Sister María Rosa said. "They gave themselves, heart and soul, to Sociedad Amigos de los Niños when we could not even pay them a decent salary or any social security."

Unlike restricted donations to SAN, the funds from this organization can be directed by Sister María Rosa to whatever use she wants. Its current ventures include the Mini Market La Zarza in Miraflores, which sells food to all SAN projects; agricultural project Flor Azul, which grows sweet potatoes, pumpkins, beans, and corn to sell to groceries and WalMart; and culinary project La Cocina de Sor, an industrial kitchen.

"Sister's dream was always to provide food for everyone," noted Quique Rodriguez, board secretary for Fundación Asistencial María Rosa. "We just put a business model on it. She loved to cook for the groups and for special occasions. Now our biggest multi-year contract is feeding nearly a thousand lunches each day to the workers who are building the new U.S. Embassy."

As her foundation began taking up more of her time, Sister María Rosa finally retreated a bit from daily decision-making for SAN's social programs: its children's homes, schools, and clinic. If she had wanted, she could have withdrawn from the urban poverty and corruption of Tegucigalpa completely to a quiet life of prayer, living out her days in tranquility in Wisconsin, in her beloved religious community. She would never retire, though. Nor would she leave Honduras—not when she felt far from finished with her work. If you tried to discuss retirement and all her accomplishments for the poor in Honduras, she deftly turned the conversation to what she still had left to do. She maintained a long list of people she urgently wanted to help: the homeless living on the streets of Tegucigalpa, the sick and elderly poor, and young single mothers.

"I have been told that 87,000 children have passed through here," Sister María Rosa said. "I told them, 'Don't tell me any more.' And why did I say that? Because I am ashamed that there are still children in the streets and in the prisons, too. Some little ones have already killed people. I can't feel very happy with what I've done because there are three times that amount we haven't reached yet."

Increasingly confronted with her own mortality, Sister María Rosa began commissioning others to take on her mission and expand her reach and influence. She urged the mission groups to represent her and SAN beyond Honduras when they return home.

"You think it's nice to come here to Honduras and help people, but now go look around you where you live," she told the groups. "Knock on your elderly neighbor's door and see what they need. That would be a good blessing for you, and you would be our extension so Sociedad could be there. I wish I could go take care of your elderly people because you have done lots of things for us.

"So stand me where I cannot go. This is my joy of the evangelic! I don't want to keep God's grace down here in Honduras. The world is one world—God's holy world. This work doesn't need a passport!"

Sister María Rosa met Pope John Paul II at the Vatican in 2004

Sister María Rosa on the field with her beloved Motagua *fútbol* team

PROFILE: THE CEO WHO COUNSELED SISTER MARÍA ROSA ON AN EXIT STRATEGY

Chameli Naraine

Chameli Naraine and Sister María Rosa met when the nun was 84 and Naraine 52, with timing so perfect that Sister María Rosa might have proclaimed it was God's plan. Naraine might not have, since she is an atheist. She is also a feminist and a CEO in banking and IT service management. Naraine and this nun from Honduras had seemingly little in common, but she and Sister María Rosa discovered a close kinship as women in charge, and Naraine's succession advice came at the precise moment that Sister María Rosa needed to hear it.

Born in Guyana of Indian descent, Naraine left South America at age 16 when her parents and four young siblings moved to Ontario, Canada. They arrived in their new home with only C$500. Naraine's father died a few years later and all the children had to chip in to support the family. As many immigrant children do, they worked hard, studied hard, and succeeded in good jobs to excel *as the first generation in a new country, all with the desire that after they rebuilt their own family, they would give back to those less fortunate.*

"My view is that I've had enough good things in life that it's time to give back," Naraine explained. "Before banking, I started in a technical career, then went into manufacturing. I've worked all over the world. Enough is enough money. After a while, what do we do with it?"

Naraine started her own charitable foundation in 2008. "Everything I give is my own personal income," she noted. "I do not fundraise. I work for the money and I give it away to my family and my foundation. I would never give money away unless I can see what I am doing with it, unless I spend time on the ground. Any organization I support has to have high integrity, value, and be a group that I trust and can see is making a real difference."

In 2008, Naraine met Jim McCallum and David Cain of Friends of Honduran Children Canada through their common tax lawyer. They hit it off, and that summer Naraine sent her mother, Padma, and a friend, Ginny Bosomworth, to Honduras to check out SAN. It was an emotional trip during which the two women and McCallum traveled with a SAN social worker into the mountains to remove four children from their indigent mother.

Padma in particular recognized SAN's extraordinary challenges: In Canada she had worked in childcare for 25 years and was familiar with the hard lives and immediate needs of children at risk. When she saw that the school in Nuevo Paraíso had run out of food she insisted on donating all their cash to buy beans, rice, and corn-meal for the school.

"She used to babysit children at a jail in Canada during visiting time, so Sister's story of getting the children out of the prisons really resonated with her," Naraine said.

After that trip, Naraine began supporting SAN, and then visited for herself in 2010 and 2011. She came to check out SAN's projects, but did not expect to find instant rapport with Sister María Rosa. She discovered very quickly that she could offer Sister María Rosa unique and rare advice as one female leader to another.

"I told her that when I am running a large company, when I am worrying about 5,000 people across the United States and Canada, I have a different set of responsibilities than everyone else does," Naraine said. "Then I told her, 'You are a CEO, too, and you have to think like one.'"

Naraine counseled Sister María Rosa on her leadership, her legacy, and an exit strategy—a succession plan for handing over daily operations of SAN to her people.

"I told Sister that she didn't have anyone in the organization to take over for her and that her donors were worried," Naraine recalled. "I also told her she should speak to her people about her values. What makes an organization good is its cleanliness, its ethics. I told her that she didn't want to embody what her government does, but rather be a role model to her people. She had to look the members of SAN's Executive Council in the eyes and tell them her values. In every situation they should learn to think, What would Sister do?"

Sister María Rosa at 84 had begun to think about the future of SAN without her leadership. But she had few peers with whom to talk frankly: Naraine and McCallum were among that small group of people who could tell Sister María Rosa like it is and advise her in such a direct way.

Naraine is candid to the point of being blunt. Sister María Rosa once invited her to breakfast to discuss a trip report Naraine had composed and left, unsolicited, on the computer in Sister María Rosa's office. Naraine's friend Bosomworth described the scene: "Chameli was sitting next to Sister at the table and said, 'Let me see your feet.' It shocked everyone. But Chameli insisted. She told Sister, 'I'd like to examine the situation, Boss. You are the CEO and the

CEO has to be healthy.' So Sister put her red, swollen legs up and Chameli started rubbing them. Then Chameli said to Sister, 'What are you going to do about this problem? If I give to an organization and you are the boss, I want you to be healthy.' And Sister said, 'I'm not worried. The Lord will take care of everything.' And Chameli replied, 'Perhaps. But I think the Guy Upstairs could use a little human backup here.'"

Naraine believes she and Sister María Rosa shared common qualities and values: They were both visionary, determined, strong leaders and exceptional judges of character who were willing to ask other people for help. Sister María Rosa might have prayed where Naraine would rely on logic and planning, but they both had a knack for understanding what works and what doesn't within the developing world.

"Sister María Rosa's projects worked in spite of Honduras," Naraine said. "What she accomplished in spite of corruption, manipulation, theft, and dictatorship is amazing. Her hard life as a child allowed her to steer the future of very poor children into hope and a richer life as productive adults. She proved that the cycle of deep poverty and deep despair can be broken and that a new beginning for a child is possible.

"Fifty years is quite an enterprise. She started small, but had a huge impact. It's so worthy."

PROFILE: THE REBELLIOUS KID WHO LEARNED TO LOVE HIS COUNTRY AND SERVE ITS PEOPLE

Claudio Pompeyo Elvir Fontecha

Claudio Pompeyo ("Cato") Elvir Fontecha was a very good student in his youth in Honduras, attending Elvel School, one of the country's best bilingual institutions. His relationship with his family wasn't so great, however. He isolated himself from his brother, sisters, and parents, preferring to spend time out drinking with friends. Sometimes he didn't go home for several days, even when his parents had grounded him.

"My father was a very strict person trying to tame a rebel kid," Elvir explained.

After graduating from Elvel, he attended the National Autonomous University of Honduras and studied communications for two years until he left to take a special Microsoft course in computer repair and networks. During that course he worked at a supermarket warehouse, where one day his coworker Geovany Herrera asked Elvir if he could help a friend with a computer problem. Herrera took him to a house in Colonia Miraflores.

"And there was Sister María Rosa, sitting at her table, very angry because she couldn't play her favorite computer game, Solitaire," Elvir laughed. Twenty minutes later, he had fixed her computer. She thanked him and resumed her game. SAN had just begun to acquire computers for some of its work, and in the following weeks Elvir fielded many calls from Sister María Rosa to come back and help her people troubleshoot computer problems. Finally, she offered him a job.

"One day she called me in to her office for a meeting and said they needed a full-time computer tech to help them, but that she couldn't pay me that much," Elvir said. "I decided I was tired of waking up at 4 a.m. to go work at the market and a restaurant and deal with customers and cooks. So I went to SAN the next day and started working with Sister."

What would have remained a very narrow, technical position at SAN exploded into much more responsibility once Sister learned Elvir was bilingual. His English is excellent. "After several years doing computers at SAN, Sister asked me to help interpret for a group of teachers from Indianapolis," Elvir remembered. "I felt fantastic after that week and was really glad Sister sent me. Then she started sending me more and more to help translate for the mission groups and medical brigades."

Today he works with most of the university groups and mission teams from Canada and the United States, coordinating construction projects, repairs on the children's homes, and all logistics for food, education, and medical brigades. During COVID, when the groups couldn't come to Honduras, he delivered and installed donated water filters to isolated rural communities, among other projects.

Elvir feels he is making a difference not just for the English-speaking groups who want to do projects for the mission and build relationships with Hondurans, but for the Hondurans themselves in remote villages and rural towns who benefit from the brigades. "I really like to go with the medical teams up into the mountains," he said. "I think my vocation is helping people up there."

Working with the North Americans, leading brigades and work projects, was not a career this once-defiant kid ever imagined for himself. He said, however, that Sister María Rosa kept working little by little to change him. "She succeeded and made me into a person who loves his country, loves his people, and respects all the people that come to help our country," he declared.

"I used to go to her house in the morning just to say hi," Elvir grinned. "One day we were chatting and I asked her why she kept me in the organization, since I was a rebel and since I wasn't even Catholic. She told me the only reason she kept me is because she could see my heart."

Elvir likes to say that despite the fact that Sister María Rosa had very little education, she had the mind of a diplomat, an economist, and a public-relations guru all in one. He says she taught him that a material reward doesn't matter all that much when it comes to helping people.

"She always taught me about the satisfaction of just a hug from people," he said. "The smile of a kid or an old person is a reward much greater than money. She also taught me that we can't always help people ourselves, but we can at least show others how to help them. That's what I try to do with the groups."

PROFILE: THE BUSINESSPEOPLE WHO COMMISSIONED AN ARTISTIC FILM

Nick and Colleen D'Angelo

By their third mission trip to Honduras, Nick and Colleen D'Angelo could no longer ignore a nagging feeling that they were called to do more than sponsor children and go on annual mission trips. For Nick, that calling began nine months before he ever set foot in Honduras.

"I was driving my oldest daughter to Ohio State for freshman orientation in June 2009," he said. "I suddenly had a thought about helping orphans. I remember thinking that was a really strange and random thought. Then, in the fall, our son asked to go on his high school's mission trip to Honduras. So he and I both went in March of 2010 and we met Sister María Rosa. And I wondered: Has anyone seen her story? Someone's got to tell this story."

Colleen went on the Gilmour Academy school mission trip the

following March. She came home also saying, "We've got to do something more. But what?"

A month later, Nick was filing through the security line at Nashville International Airport when he started a conversation with the gentleman behind him.

"On business trips I usually just keep my head down, but for whatever reason I started talking with the man," Nick remembered. "He told me his son was an aspiring filmmaker who was heading off to film a Christian mission in Africa. And I said, 'That is so weird. I have a story I want to tell and I need a young filmmaker like that to tell it.' He gave me his son's card and that was how we heard about Dave Altizer."

Their first attempt to reach Altizer and pitch Sister María Rosa's story was unsuccessful. Then life got busy and they shelved their idea for a year or two. During that time, Nick and Colleen began to doubt their ability to take on something as creative and artistic as a film. "We were feeling like: Who are we to do this? I've been in insurance for 30 years, and Colleen was in medical sales marketing," said Nick. "None of that is creative at all. We're not filmmakers."

Then another trip to Honduras in 2014 with their younger daughter stirred the pot.

"At that point Sister was getting elderly, and we didn't know how long she would be with us," said Colleen. "We just had to do this. When you hear Sister talk, you are absolutely drawn to do more for the organization. We were."

Colleen found Altizer's website and looked at his work on Vimeo. His uplifting African mission film convinced her that he was meant for this work in Honduras. So she private-messaged him on Facebook. She says she and Nick were ready to look for another filmmaker if he didn't respond, but Altizer answered almost immediately: Could they meet him in Nashville to discuss it? By coincidence,

KATHY MARTIN O'NEIL

*the D'Angelos' oldest daughter lived in Nashville, so during a
Christmas 2014 visit, they met with Altizer to present their idea.*

*In July 2015, Nick and Colleen brought Altizer and another
filmmaker, Nick Serban IV, to SAN to shoot what would become a
35-minute documentary. In five days they filmed Sister María Rosa
and visited all of SAN's projects. They interviewed current SAN
leaders and elderly Hondurans who had worked with Sister María
Rosa back in her La Policlínica days. They shot footage of a teen
group from Gilmour Academy laying bricks that week to build a
security wall around Nuevo Paraíso and filmed a short fundraising
video for a CrowdRise campaign where the D'Angelos's daughter
and her friends appealed for child sponsors to help support 15 babies
newly arrived at Nuevo Paraíso.*

*Back home, Altizer and Serban excerpted some of their footage
to craft a short video for Sister María Rosa to use on a visit back to
the School Sisters of Saint Francis in Milwaukee. They finished the
documentary, titled* We See Her, *in 2020. The D'Angelos hope that
SAN's North American partner organizations and mission groups
can utilize the film for marketing, development, church appeals, and
movie premiere fundraisers. The only stipulation is that 100 percent
of the money raised has to go to SAN.*

*The D'Angelos are a little awestruck that their imperative to
help Sister María Rosa resulted in something so creative, so out of
their realm as businesspeople. Their hope is that this film will spread
word of SAN and Sister María Rosa's life to wider audiences
beyond the mission travelers who come to Nuevo Paraíso.*

*"It's so surprising," said Colleen. "We're really not like this in
everyday life. But here in Honduras we just let God's plan unfold."*

*Nick agreed. "God absolutely told us to do this," he said. "We had
to do this because someone, somehow, out of the blue on the freeway
between Cleveland and Columbus, told me to go help orphans. The*

only orphans I had ever encountered before that were the Little Rascals on television."

There was something about Sister María Rosa and SAN, they said, that just took hold in their lives.

"When you heard Sister María Rosa speak, she challenged you to do more than you thought you could do," said Colleen. "How could you not want to be part of something like that?"

CHAPTER 12

TRIBUTES FOR 50 YEARS OF LOVING CHILDREN

SISTER MARÍA ROSA REFLECTS ON HER LEGACY

--"I never had a lot of money, but I have a big mouth to pray!"--

On November 21, 2016, La Basílica Menor de Nuestra Patrona la Virgen de Suyapa in Tegucigalpa was surrounded by media vans. Inside the cavernous church, bright morning sun gleamed through the towering stained-glass windows and tall open-air doorways, and birds and breezes flew in and out at will. Television cameramen loitered atop pews and platforms, staking out their vantage points, while reporters consulted their phones. Members of the National Congress, Honduran dignitaries, benefactors from the United States and Canada, current and past children of SAN, and various friends and family of Sister María Rosa milled up and down the center aisle, greeting each other. On the ornate altar, the heels of priests and servers clicked the marble floor as the men lit candles and prepared vessels for Communion.

All this commotion was in preparation for Sister María Rosa's 90th birthday Mass. She would have called it a "holy commotion," but no one was sure if she would attend her own celebration; she had been sick for several weeks with a stomach ailment. Her staff had considered cancelling the Mass or at least the luncheon to follow. There was more at stake that morning than a birthday party, however: After Mass, Sister María Rosa would be decorated by the National Congress with the Gran Cruz con Placa de Oro (the Great Gold Cross), Honduras's highest distinction for service to the country.

Promptly at 10 a.m. there was a hubbub of activity at the Basilica's south entrance. Sister María Rosa had arrived. Wearing a white dress and black veil and smiling hugely from her wheelchair, she looked well, though thinner and a little tired. She didn't get far inside the door before she was surrounded by adults and children, who quickly formed a line to give her a hug or gentle kiss of greeting. Then the reporters moved in to interview her. They were polite and deferential, stooping down next to her wheelchair to ask her questions, but they thrust competing microphones in her face. She told me the next morning that she had never experienced a media frenzy like that before.

After a rash of reunions among Sister María Rosa and her admirers, Geovany Herrera, a grown child of SAN employed at Sister María Rosa's foundation, wheeled her chair to the first row of pews and parked it along the center aisle. The National Congress representatives, including Deputy Vice President Gladis Aurora López, sat near the front, and all other guests took seats behind them and Sister María Rosa. The Mass began, concelebrated by Father Carlo Magno Nuñez, pastor of the Basilica, and three other priests, each of whom gave a homily about Sister María Rosa's important role in their lives. (Cardinal Rodriguez had been invited—he is an old friend of Sister María Rosa's—but was unavailable.) Children from SAN's Pedro Atala homes read the scripture readings and sang in a small choir led by Santa Barahona, a Pedro Atala teacher and musician. Throughout the service, cameramen continued to dart around the church, dangling microphones in front of Sister María Rosa whenever she sang or prayed.

After the Mass came the award ceremony. Sister María Rosa's chair was wheeled to the foot of the altar and turned to face the congregation. After a short speech, Deputy Vice President López draped a blue and white sash over Sister María Rosa's shoulders and pinned the Gran Cruz con Placa de Oro cross onto it. Our applause went on for a long time, echoing loudly from the church's high ceilings. Standing just behind Sister María Rosa was Audelia Rodríguez, a grown child of SAN now working in the National Congress. Sister María Rosa reached up several times to grasp her hand.

The Gran Cruz con Placa de Oro award, founded in 1941, is granted to Hondurans and foreigners by the president for "eminent services rendered to the country, by important benefits granted to humanity, or by notorious merits in the field of culture." Former awardees include Hugo Chavez, Fidel Castro, and several past presidents of Honduras. The medal itself is stunning, adorned with symbols of Honduras's history and pride. This award is the highest of six grades that make up the Order of Francisco Morazán, named for the Honduran hero, general, and president of the 19th-century Federal Republic of Central America.

Sister María Rosa beamed at the thundering applause. As usual she gathered strength from an enthusiastic audience.

As the clapping waned, she suddenly began to speak in a loud, hoarse, commanding voice. The reporters ran forward and formed a tight circle of bodies, cameras, and microphones around her.

She directed comments first to Honduran children.

"Children! Don't stay on the streets," she announced in Spanish. "Come! I will take care of you!"

Then she made an appeal to the National Congress.

"Please think when you make the laws," she said. "Don't do it without asking the Holy Spirit for the grace of wisdom to know how to make good things with God's direction."

She paused and then added an afterthought.

"God created the Ten Commandments in stone, and nobody can erase those!" she declared. Some friends told me later that they wondered if she was slyly referring to the seven articles of the Honduran Constitution that are considered "set in stone" and unchangeable—a political flashpoint over several recent elections. Sister María Rosa quickly went on, however, to recommend that parliamentary officials give *un miradita,* a little look, to the Commandments so that God might enlighten them in their actions for the benefit of all Hondurans.

When she concluded, Sister María Rosa was wheeled down the Basilica's center aisle and outside onto the terrace, interrupted by greetings and hugs every few feet. Outside the church, 50 children from her SAN projects sang for her and released dozens of white balloons to soar over the barrios and the high-rises of Tegucigalpa.

A birthday luncheon at Hacienda el Trapiche restaurant followed, including cake and a steel drum band that lured many guests to the dance floor. Sister María Rosa sat at the head table with Fernando Aragón, SAN's board president;

Doctor Enrique Aguilar de Paz, her boss from her La Policlínica days; and a representative of DINAF, the government's department of child and family services. A program of announcements included songs and birthday cards from her children at SAN's Nuevo Paraíso, Santiago Apóstol, and Pedro Atala homes, a poem by Doctor Aguilar de Paz, words of appreciation from Aragón and the agent from DINAF, and a gift from Friends of Honduran Children Indiana of an annual $5,000 Health and Wellness Fund to cover children's medical needs as they arise. The festivities concluded with a heartfelt performance by Quique Rodríguez of *"Un Clavel para una Rosa* (A Carnation for a Rose)," the song he wrote for Sister María Rosa: *"Tu que tienes el alma sensitiva, cómo el suave perfume de una rosa, y que ocultas en el alma la pureza, cómo oculta la violeta su tristeza, de su suave y delicada florecilla* (You have such a sensitive soul, like a soft scent of a rose, like a violet concealing sadness in its soft and delicate flower, you conceal the pureness of your soul)."

Sister María Rosa's stamina that day was astounding. After a month in bed, she looked like she could revel in this celebration forever. She addressed the luncheon crowd with an open-mouthed smile of excitement and delight.

"I did not understand everything that happened today. Where did all those cameras come from?" Sister María Rosa grinned. "But I know this means that everybody is happy about the work of Sociedad Amigos de los Niños, which belongs to God.

"I am thankful for a lot of people, because Sociedad Amigos de los Niños is not the work of María Rosa. In the beginning we had so much help from friends like Don Pedro [Atala], Don Salomón [Kafati], Don Rafael [Ferrari], Don Miguel [Facussé], and Don Manuel [Villeda Toledo.] María

Rosa alone cannot do anything; she is just a woman like everyone else! You all—and many who are already in heaven —have supported me. You have helped me and you had faith in my work. Go and see the work to see what can be accomplished in Honduras. It's not all about money. Money is necessary, but what is more important is the attention and love that one can give to children."

છ૪ૐ

O N SOME DAYS DURING HER FINAL YEARS, SISTER MARÍA Rosa could restrain herself from weighing in on the daily minutiae of running her foundation and SAN; on other days she could not help getting involved. "I am not dead yet," she was fond of warning her staff. She called herself "an emergency woman" who still loved "a holy commotion" and was ready to take whatever challenge God sent her from whoever knocked at the door.

"I am never afraid; I still go at things," she insisted. "If I have to cross a big mountain, I go there. That's probably why I can't walk anymore."

She said she could not live without doing this work. "My religious community says, 'You are already of age. You must come here to us; you should be resting,'" she said. "But I tell them, 'When the Lord wants me to rest, He will take me to my eternal rest.' As long as I have life and a drop of blood in my body, I will keep going, *sigue adelante!* Because my life is for the people until the Lord calls me and says, 'María Rosa, mission complete.'"

In her nineties, Sister María Rosa harbored no worries about the future of SAN. She told me once that she woke up from a midmorning doze to hear lots of children playing and shouting nearby. She immediately thought, *I know in my heart very strongly that God will not let this project die.*

"God says, 'Let the children come to me.' These children go into your heart and your mind," Sister María Rosa assured me. "That's why our project is so grace-filled. The children are the ones who motivate the people to help. They are God —the little ones. Even some of the big ones!"

In the midst of Honduras's endemic violence, poverty, and epic class struggles, she held on to the conviction that the hope-filled outlook of SAN's children would result in a brighter future for her country's poor people.

"So full of love, these kids in their Holy Hour pray for the parent who has abused them, " she noted. "They are not the poorest of the poor anymore. Nobody here goes without food, clothes, and studies. Sometimes my kids will give away a toy if they have too many, saying, 'This is for the poor.' Because they have food, school, housemothers, everything, they forget that they are the poor."

She pointed out that her children have learned how to love and help and care about other people because they themselves had been loved. "We are the poor," she continued. "We have to be just."

Although Sister María Rosa said often that her children don't owe anything back to SAN, she did pray that they would grow up with a vocation for service. With intention, SAN has always trained its children to have a conscience about the needs of others. She hoped they would go out as adults and extend to everyone they encounter the mercy they were shown in their upbringing, even to the families who failed them.

"My children would ask me, 'Why did I have to come here? Where are my parents?'" she said. "I did not criticize their parents. I told them, 'Your parents did not have this place to come to and train themselves well. But here you will train well and as soon as you can, go help them.'"

She often sang a song with her children and volunteers, her lilting soprano rising above the buzzy mumbles of her teenage boys, that distilled her prayer to God for simplicity in a complicated world. The lyrics repeat one of her deepest desires: "I want to have the heart of a child."

Padre, Padre, Padre, Padre,
　　Yo quiero tener un corazón de niño,
　　Yo quiero tener un corazón de niño,
　　Yo quiero tener un corazón de niño,
　　Para amarte mas.
　　Un corazón abierto,
　　Un corazón sincero,
　　Un corazón fraterno,
　　Un corazón bien simple.
　　Padre, Padre, Padre, Padre.

Father, Father, Father, Father,
　　I want to have the heart of a child,
　　I want to have the heart of a child,
　　I want to have the heart of a child,
　　To give more love to You.
　　An open heart,
　　A sincere heart,
　　A brotherly heart,
　　A simple heart.
　　Father, Father, Father, Father.

Sister María Rosa received the *Gran Cruz con Placa de Oro*
award from the Honduran government

PROFILE: THE CHEF WHO ANSWERED THE CALL TO A RELIGIOUS VOCATION

Reverend Hector Mateus-Ariza

Hector Mateus-Ariza is convinced he would never have become a priest if not for Sister María Rosa.

"God took me to her to show me what to do with my life," he declared.

The energetic black-haired pastor serving today in the Baltimore, Maryland, archdiocese grew up in poverty in Colombia. He started working in restaurants at age seven to help support his family and by 27 was cooking for the president of Colombia and his cabinet. He questioned his purpose, though: What was his life really about?

"So I quit that job and went to Honduras to visit my friend Gabriel—the only friend I knew in another country," Mateus-Ariza said. "I wanted to feel life outside my country."

Doctor Gabriel Colorado lived in a house in Sister María Rosa's

Miraflores compound; he was her personal physician for decades. When Mateus-Ariza arrived in Tegucigalpa, Sister María Rosa and her driver picked him up at the airport. She told him she had an idea for a project: She wanted a chef to teach cooking and nutrition to young women at her new Reyes Irene Valenzuela school for teenage domestic workers.

"I said yes right away. And then I started cooking for Sister, too, spending every night with her and Gabriel playing cards, asking lots of questions about SAN, and listening to her stories about the hurricanes and other great challenges," Mateus-Ariza remembered. "I was so fascinated by all that she had gone through in her life. I thought it was amazing that she woke up so early every morning to pray; I decided that prayer really works!"

During his year in Honduras, Mateus-Ariza said he suddenly and surprisingly found himself very happy. "I didn't have anything in particular to be happy for: girlfriend or job or money," he said. "For the first time, the source of my happiness was not somewhere else; it didn't exist outside myself. It was a state of mind. Happiness only became a reality for me when I was sharing what I had to give with others."

One Sunday Mateus-Ariza went to a Mass celebrated by Tegucigalpa's archbishop, Cardinal Rodríguez. "I can't explain it, but afterward in the night I woke up feeling different," Mateus-Ariza said. "I was thinking that for the first time in my life everything was in place. I thought, 'I am fully happy and now I can leave.'"

As he thought about what he calls "that weird night," he telephoned a U.S. priest friend who had once worked in Colombia. The priest had invited Mateus-Ariza to come to the seminary in the United States, but he had said no. As a child of a poor family, he had never wanted to take a vow of poverty as a priest.

"I told my friend that I felt different since that Mass but at 29 I was too old to become a priest," Mateus-Ariza said. "Then he said

that somebody from his diocese had actually called him the previous night, looking for Latino candidates to the priesthood. I told him no again—I said I didn't know enough English, it would be too hard to get a visa from Colombia, and I didn't even have a paying job."

Nonetheless, Mateus-Ariza decided to try. The seminary sent him a visa request to present to the U.S. embassy in his hometown of Bogotá. As he expected, he was denied the visa. After his rejection Mateus-Ariza waited near the agents' windows to help another visa applicant who was not from Bogotá to find his way around. Suddenly one of the agents motioned Mateus-Ariza to come back to the window.

"He asked for my passport and then he just gave me the visa!" he laughed, shrugging his shoulders.

Mateus-Ariza returned to Honduras to tell Sister María Rosa he was leaving. "She was really sad, and I hated making her sad," he said. "She told me she couldn't have let me go for any other reason but this. She couldn't fight this." Sister María Rosa even flew back to Colombia with Mateus-Ariza to help him buy and pack winter clothes for the United States.

"My mother couldn't believe how Sister knew exactly what I needed: jacket, hat, gloves," said Mateus-Ariza. "She said she couldn't believe somebody else could love her son so much."

The seminary was challenging, and Mateus-Ariza said that at least once he wanted to quit and go back to Honduras, not home to Colombia. Nine years later, he was ordained a priest in the archdiocese of Baltimore, one of a group of the first Latino priests to be ordained there in 200 years.

"Sister María Rosa must have been praying very hard, since all her prayers were always answered," grinned Mateus-Ariza. "How that simple woman could sit at her table and solve so many immediate problems for people was amazing! When I was in Honduras, we would be driving somewhere and she would see a little kid on a

bridge sniffing glue and she'd say, 'We need to find something for that kid. We need to find a place for boys like him—we can make a place, a property somewhere.' And if I said, 'No we can't, there's no room,' she would just say, 'Well, maybe I don't know how to do everything, but that's why I have you. I don't know how, but just do it.'

"Then, right before I left, she founded the Pedro Atala homes. Those houses were not so nice in the beginning. I said, 'But Sister, we have to wait to start this project till we have donors or volunteers.' And she said, 'We cannot leave those kids in jails with their mothers; it breaks my heart! I am going now! I don't care if we are not prepared. What's worse: to have those kids live in these houses or stay in jail?'"

Mateus-Ariza says his faith makes sense today because of Sister María Rosa.

"She could put all this together because she was completely convinced that she was on this planet to take care of the people of God, especially those most in need," he said. "I find when I talk now about Jesus, it's easy for me. It's like talking about somebody I knew very well. I'm not trying to make Sister into Jesus, but what she did in her life is what Jesus did two thousand years ago."

PROFILE: THE INTERNATIONAL COUPLE
WHOSE MATCH WAS MADE BY SISTER
MARÍA ROSA

John and Alby Glassmeyer

John and Alby Glassmeyer of Cleveland recently celebrated their 17th wedding anniversary. The American businessman and the Colombian Spanish teacher met 20 or so years ago in Honduras and credit their union to the matchmaking talent and dogged determination of Sister María Rosa.

Alba Cecilia Mateus-Ariza, or Alby, had come to Tegucigalpa from Bogotá for what she thought would be a monthlong project helping SAN and visiting her brother, Hector Mateus-Ariza, who was working as a chef for Sister María Rosa. She ended up staying much longer. She said her life at that time wasn't very happy. "At age 32, I was feeling too old to meet anyone and fall in love," she said. "My grandma used to say that by age 21 you need to be married; otherwise you're going to be single all your life."

John first met Alby when he came to Tegucigalpa in 2001 on a mission trip with Church of the Gesu in University Heights, Ohio, outside Cleveland. "I was relatively new at a job and had had a rough time for 18 months," he explained. "I was severely burned out, and suddenly the crazy notion that Father Lorn Snow kept bringing up about going to Honduras stopped seeming so crazy. I figured I would go on the trip and work with orphans. If that didn't put your mind right, what would?"

In Honduras, John noticed Alby right away, though it took several more mission trips for Alby to notice John. He asked for her email address in February 2003 as he boarded the group bus to leave for the airport and home. On the bus, he asked Mae Valenzuela about Alby and her life. Intrigued, Valenzuela brought his interest to Sister María Rosa, who wanted to know all about John: Was he married? What was he like? By the time John returned to Honduras in June the matchmaking wheels were in motion.

"At every turn, Sister was making sure Alby was available to be with me," John recalled. "It didn't matter what work Alby was doing. Sister would arrange for her to be with me wherever I was."

"I was working in the office at the time," Alby added. "And Sister would call me and say, 'Come to my table for lunch.' And I would tell her, 'No, I need to work.' And she would say, 'I don't care! Come eat lunch right now.' And John would be there."

When the Cleveland group saw John and Alby sitting together one evening at Valenzuela's cousin's hacienda, trying to communicate over glasses of wine, they began to suspect romance. The next morning, breakfast was set at several tables of four, with just one table set for two. When a pair of children tried to sit at the special table, they were tapped on the shoulder and escorted away so that John and Alby could sit together in that cozy spot.

"So many things were staged for us!" exclaimed John.

Soon after, John made a weeklong trip to Honduras for the sole purpose of spending time with Alby. One lunchtime when Sister

María Rosa and Alby were talking in Spanish, he noticed Alby looking more and more uncomfortable, even distressed. "I didn't understand a word of what these two women were saying. I was just eating my lunch," *he remembered.* "But Alby seemed boxed into a corner and close to tears. So I looked up at them. And Sister said to me in English, 'You are not young people and you are not getting any younger. You should just get married right now.'"

John said he was about to turn this declaration around on her. "I thought I'd joke and say, 'Sure, let's get married right this minute!' But then I thought, maybe she has her friend Father Max hiding in a closet ready to do this!" *he recalled.* "So I didn't say anything." Back in Cleveland he phoned Alby and asked her what she thought of that conversation. Alby told him, "If Sister says we should get married, then I think we should."

John arrived in Honduras on Christmas Eve to surprise Alby with a ring, but the secret was too hard for the Hondurans to keep. Sister María Rosa had teased Alby that she would "be so happy on Christmas" when a woman from Cleveland would arrive with her Christmas gift from John. Alby had asked who was coming, but Sister María Rosa had waved her off with "Oh, don't bother me, asking those details!"

John proposed to Alby on the couch in Sister María Rosa's living area. All the other people had left the room, but Sister María Rosa stayed, playing Solitaire on the computer, with the TV on. She told them, "You two just sit and visit with one another. Pretend like I'm not even here." After Alby said yes she took the ring over to show Sister María Rosa, who declared happily, "Yes, I already know!"

John and Alby credit their marriage to Sister María Rosa's matchmaking. Alby calls their union one of Sister's miracles.

"When I would say that she makes miracles in people's lives, Sister would say, 'No, I am just a channel that God uses to help people,'" *Alby noted.* "But there have been so many miracles from

Sister María Rosa in my family: in my own life, in my brother becoming a priest, even in the way she talked to and forgave my father, just before he died, for things that had happened in our family."

"Well, as a channel or not," John added, "she brought someone incredible into my life. She said the right things at the right time to get us to think in that way."

Alby said Sister María Rosa also taught her how to be happy.

"She told me once when I was feeling separated from my family in another country that you need to learn to be happy with what you have," Alby said. "She taught me not to need what I do not have. And that's what she taught her children: to do something with their lives, to go out and be professional and not repeat the bad history or unhappiness. She gave so much opportunity for people to go on in life, be happy, and be better. She really was a channel; for me being close to her was like being close to heaven or God."

CHAPTER 13

MISSION ACCOMPLISHED

SISTER MARÍA ROSA IS CALLED THE ANGEL OF THE POOR

--"Christ said, 'Pick up your cross and follow Me.'
He didn't say to drag it and complain!"--

On October 16, 2020, at 4 p.m., another crowd gathered hastily in Tegucigalpa's Basilica to celebrate Sister María Rosa. Earlier that day, SAN had published this announcement:

With deep sorrow we communicate that today she handed her soul to the Divine Redeemer, our mother:

Sor María Rosa Leggol (1926-2020)

An exemplary Honduran who with her unwavering faith, her strength, her passion for serving others and her aura of holiness leaves us a legacy to continue transforming the lives of those most in need; a symbol of love, trust and mercy that leaves a deep mark in our hearts

"Let the little children come to me, and do not hinder them; for the kingdom of heaven belongs to such as these." Matthew 19:14

Sister María Rosa had come through a short hospitalization with COVID-19 in July, but the treatment took a toll on the 93-year-old, already in failing health. After an October hospitalization for pre-existing non-alcoholic hepatic cirrhosis, during which the Honduran media urged healing prayers from the entire country, she spent her final days in her own bed at home, surrounded by loved ones from her biological family and her SAN family. Cardinal Rodriguez came and administered the sacrament of the Anointing of the Sick. Quique Rodriguez played guitar, and she even sang with him at times; music was always a very special form of communication for them.

"She was leaving us little by little, not all at once, because she didn't want us to suffer," he said. "She told Pancho Paz that she wouldn't leave suddenly, but would give us three days to prepare before she really left. From the time the doctor told us her dying had begun to the time she died was exactly 72 hours!"

She died at 9:24 a.m. on October 16. Cardinal Rodriguez celebrated her funeral Mass that same afternoon. A large congregation of Sister María Rosa's family, friends, benefactors, and current and grown children attended, along with many priests and nuns. At least one local television station broadcast not only the funeral but the slow procession through Tegucigalpa traffic of the white van carrying her casket as it made its way from her own Miraflores chapel to the Basilica. At the conclusion of the Mass, many of her children and supporters gave speeches from the pulpit, unwilling to end the celebration of her life.

"I got up and told everyone, 'Just think on Mom every day,'" said Quique Rodriguez. "I told them to choose the best wall in their house and keep a picture of her there to look at every day and teach their kids about the person in that picture."

In conclusion, her children lined the roadway leading away from the Basilica and released white balloons silently into the darkening sky as Sister María Rosa was laid to rest in Tegucigalpa's Jardines de Paz Suyapa (Gardens of Peace) cemetery.

Santa Súbita! (Sudden Saint!) proclaimed the front page of *Suyapa Medios Fides* newspaper in Tegucigalpa the next day. Headlines in this and other newspapers declared, "Thank You for Everything, Sor María Rosa!" "Angel of the Children and Mother of Honduras!" "Opening a possibility for the first Honduran saint!" "A legacy of dedication, humility and service in favor of the children of Honduras!" Sister María Rosa was called the Angel of the Poor and an exceptional human being, an example of love and solidarity, and a warrior who fought a thousand battles to help those most in need.

Tributes, testimonials, and tales about Sister María Rosa's work and her faith flooded forth from all walks of Honduran life, from politicians to priests, from her grown children to her current children and SAN staffers. Juan Orlando Hernández, the president of Honduras, sent this tweet: "Rest in peace, Sor María Rosa, friend of children and those in need. Amid the sadness, we are also proud that Honduras has had an exceptional daughter like her, whose example of generosity we all must emulate." General Carlos Cordero, former commissioner of COPECO, the Honduran government body that coordinates disaster relief efforts, said in a Catholic newspaper, "She cared for hundreds of families and thousands of children in precarious living conditions. Thank you, Sor María Rosa, for taking up the cross, for your love, and for your eternal yes in favor of the most vulnerable. Thank you for your love to the point of madness."

Eduardo Atala, businessman, son of Pedro Atala Simón, and a president of the national Motagua soccer team, spoke in *El Heraldo* daily newspaper about Sister María Rosa's faithfulness to the national sport. "She painted her chapel deep blue out of love for her team and when they won championships the players took the cup to the chapel to receive her blessing," he said. Padre Carlo Magno Nuñez, vicar general of the Archdiocese of Tegucigalpa, told *Suyapa Medios Fides,* "Sister María Rosa was a Eucharistic woman full of God and the Holy Spirit who let herself be carried away by Him. All those works she achieved were inspired by that same spirit. She was a self-sacrificing mother who assumed as a vocation to have many spiritual sons and daughters. It is a fermentation, an effervescence of God's love in our midst. She is a woman who undoubtedly receives the eternal prize."

Cardinal Rodriguez noted in his eulogy during Sister María Rosa's funeral Mass that despite her illness, she held a great love for Honduras in her heart until its very last beat. "I wish there were thousands of Sor María Rosas, since our country needs it," he said. He also declared to *Suyapa Medios Fides*, "Sor María Rosa fulfilled the stage and vocation that God had given her. If we have loved her during this life, now our love must be reflected in imitating her examples. Now it is up to each of us to think about what we can do to collaborate so that her work does not end. We thank God for this luminous life, because when He finds a generous heart, He can do wonders."

Many of Sister María Rosa's grown children came to attend her funeral or visited her during her illness. They shared their own gratitude for the woman who radically improved their lives.

"Today I am who I am thanks to Sor María Rosa and my aunts [housemothers] who helped me," said Marta López, who was abandoned at age one by her parents at the public hospital, where she almost died from severe malnutrition. A single mother today, she is proud that her son is about to graduate high school. "Because of her, I knew how to raise my son and set him on the path of good."

"Sor María Rosa was an angel and a great lady who was very comprehensive," said Cinthia Zepeda, a former student who became an instructor at SAN's Reyes Irene Valenzuela Institute. Zepeda arrived at SAN as a 14-year-old with a fourth-grade education. Her mother had deserted the family when Zepeda was ten, forcing the young girl to stay home and supervise her younger brothers in a dangerous neighborhood. "Sor was really good at helping people with exactly what they needed for the future," she continued. "She didn't discriminate where you came from and she always knew how to make people feel love."

"I consider Sor to be my mother and the mother of Honduras with all that love," said Aminta Margarita Navarro Herrera, whose parents and brothers were killed by thieves when she was 13. She came to SAN with her three surviving siblings. After high school, Herrera studied social work and earned three master's degrees. Today she works in the Honduran Department of Development and Cooperation as an international consultant. "What is important to me is that Sor saw us as a family and didn't spread us out," she added. "She never gave up when there were problems."

Marvin Emilio López, who came to SAN's homes at age two after his parents died, believes his life would have been very different without Sister María Rosa. "This was the best that could have happened to me: coming here and growing up with her, receiving her love and education," stated López, who owns and runs a printing press. "The contact with her was so good. She always gave us good advice, which really helped us in life."

"When I was seven years old my parents died and I came with my brothers to Sor María Rosa," said Alba Banegas, a teacher at Nuevo Paraíso's elementary school. (The school's principal, Gloria Reyes, was also raised by Sister María Rosa.) "I had the opportunity to get a degree as an elementary school teacher and ever since then I have been working with Sor."

For Arnold Avila, a grown child of SAN who supports his young family as an artist in Roatán, Sister María Rosa gave "the most sincere" love. "There was the love in her hands when she hugged me and told me to be a good person, to be simple, to be noble," he wrote on his Facebook page. "There was the love in her eyes when she saw us and believed in us that we could change our country. She was the mother's love for many Hondurans. She saw me with love since I was little. believed in me and gave me a happy life. She taught me not to repeat the story"—the bad history of the situations from which her children came.

A current university student who came to SAN as a young child after her mother died also wrote on Facebook about her second loss of a mother. "Our mother died today and she is no longer present in my life, but to her I owe all my achievements," wrote Dania Karina Servellón Garcia. "She was the one who supported me in difficult moments, the one who encouraged me when no one else did and the one who gave everything for me and many children and young people. Sor María Rosa will always live in our hearts."

SAN will go on as Sister María Rosa intended, building on both the infrastructure that she created and her mandate that her children "change their stories" and grow up with a sense of responsibility, accountability, and a desire to work rather than stay poor. With the broad shoulders of a diminutive nun on which to stand, the organization can show a 55-year track record of success, evident in the self-sufficient lives of three generations of Hondurans. Sister María Rosa gave tens of thousands of poor children a home, safety, nutrition, education, clothing, well-being, and a new family. She worked to heal the traumas of abuse and abandonment from their past, but her real project was to give them a future and a successful place in society.

"SAN will continue working for the benefit of children and adolescents in situations that violate their rights," said Carolina Agüero de Agurcia, SAN's board president. "It is unfortunate that there are still children who are victims of abuse and abandonment, who are exposed to situations of violence, and who lack the right to protection, health, home, education and food. There are still families in situations of economic and social vulnerability, extreme poverty, and unemployment. So we will need to reinforce Sister's image both locally and internationally to continue with her legacy and her spirituality. We will continue to work on spreading the word of Sister to encourage her children and youth to keep God's faith, study, and work hard to succeed in their lives and become useful to society."

Quique Rodriguez confirmed that Sister María Rosa's legacy will be secure. "It will be impossible to fill those shoes," he said. "Who's going to have the charisma? Who will be as eloquent? Who's going to have the magic? But we, her kids, will have to be a testimonial for her. It's time for us to put our feet on the ground and make her dreams come true. We'll have to find sustainable ways to continue her job in effectively, aligning with her vision and mission to fight for the most vulnerable and those who for some reason lost their parents."

৩৵৩

AT ONE POINT AMID THE SADNESS AND TEARS OF SISTER María Rosa's funeral at the Basilica, there were whoops and shouts of joy: After the Mass, Cardinal Rodriguez returned to the pulpit to announce that he would advance his friend's cause for sainthood.

"We are going to undertake the path," he smiled. "We need testimonies from all who knew her and from all who received her goodness." He asked the crowd to show their love simply by writing down what they experienced with Sister María Rosa and how she shaped their lives.

There are many steps to sainthood. There is usually a five-year waiting period to even begin the process, although that can be waived by the Pope, as Pope John Paul II did for Mother Teresa in beginning her process less than two years following her death. First, the bishop of the diocese opens an investigation into the holiness and good works of the candidate and collects witness testimonies and other evidence. If the case is accepted by the Vatican's Congregation for the Causes of Saints, the person is called a Servant of God. That group reviews the evidence of the individual's heroic virtue and if they pass it to the Pope, the person is named Venerable.

This is where miracles come in. To reach the next stage, beatification, with the title Blessed, the candidate needs to be associated with a miracle due to prayers made to that person after her death. Most common are medical miracles, unexplainable by science, where a suffering person is unexpectedly and suddenly cured of an illness. This event is seen to be granted by God by the intercession of the Venerable Servant of God. After beatification, a second miracle is required before the Pope can move forward with canonization into sainthood, unless the candidate was martyred, in which case only one miracle is required.

Sister María Rosa would be the first saint to come from Honduras and only the second Central American saint, after Óscar Romero of El Salvador. (The cause of Servant of God Casimir Cypher, killed in 1975 as a missionary in Honduras, is also being advanced, but he was born in Wisconsin.)

I asked Sister María Rosa about sainthood once or twice. She laughed and admitted that she tries to be good, but her "human side is very strong."

"I am not too obedient," she grinned mischievously. "I made vows of poverty and then chastity and then obedience. And in my mind I was thinking, *Poverty and chastity I can do, but obedience I cannot do. Except only to Him!*" jabbing upward into the air the crucifix she carried with her constantly for the last several years of her life.

"Someone once said to me, 'Don't worry, María Rosa, the saints were very hard to live with, too!'" she continued. "But I will just let God do what He wants to do with this poor woman and not worry about it. He is strong and omnipotent. I say to Him, 'Lord, I am trying to do my best but the rest is Yours. You are God!'"

She liked to say often that "María Rosa is nobody" and that God does all the work, but her own holiness was profound. She radiated God's love in her labors for the poor. Most people responded to Sister María Rosa's call on an emotional, not a rational, level. They were attracted inexorably to her spirituality, her transcendence, her direct pipeline of communication with the Creator. This put her in the company of rare spiritual leaders, as Harvard psychologist Howard Gardner describes them in his 1999 book *Intelligence Reframed*:

> *Undoubtedly, certain individuals exude a feeling of spirituality, a sense of being in touch with the cosmos, and a capacity to make those around them feel that they themselves have been touched, made to feel more whole or more themselves, or led toward an enhanced relation to the transcendent. Whatever the mechanism... this 'contact with the spiritual' constitutes an important ingredient in conveying to people the goal of their quest, and, perhaps equally important, how they might embark upon the right pathway.*

Passionate conviction—especially when it is all-in like Sister María Rosa's—is undeniably inspirational, and her zeal felt sacred. Even her own staff counted Sister María Rosa's holiness as a job benefit. "Whenever I was in prayer with her early in the morning, I would sit behind her," said Choni Enamorado, director of the Reyes Irene Valenzuela project. "That way, when God would throw all His blessings on her, maybe some would fall on me!"

In social psychology, the word "charisma" refers to a strong personality or quality that gives a person influence or authority over others. In Christian theology, a "charism" means an extraordinary spiritual grace granted by God to help a person do good works. For either definition, Sister María Rosa was the poster girl. Her charisms of courage, audacity, and fierce love for parentless children defined her. These graces found her a childhood home among the School Sisters of Saint Francis and won her the order's approval to begin her project. They willed SAN into being and kept her vision at the forefront for more than 50 years, resulting in tens of thousands of lives pivoted toward a much more hopeful and bright future. They attracted many thousands of supporters willing to donate immense time, talent, and treasure to her cause.

There is of course a flip side—a very human side—to Sister María Rosa's strong spirit and personality. While her charisma might have pulled followers irresistibly into her mission and kickstarted the talk of sainthood, her determination could sometimes translate into impatience and obstinance, even on her most prayerful days. Sister María Rosa's charism of audacity could turn her into a fierce scold of her teenagers or her grown children. Her single-minded focus on her mission could put blinders on progress and new methodologies and even the alleged crimes attributed to powerful Honduran men with whom she and SAN had beneficial friendships. Her fierce, unstoppable drive made some people whistle in wonder, though others might have called it brazen or impudent.

Goodness, however, is complex and multidimensional, and Sister María Rosa is not the first holy person in history to raise eyebrows for unusual methods or strong mannerisms. The canon of saints includes some very complicated human beings, with significant quirks standing side by side with prodigious holiness. Saint Ignatius spent two straight years in a cave praying seven hours a days. Saint Simeon Stylites the Elder lived atop a series of ever-higher pillars in the desert for 37 years. Saint Catherine of Siena had a recurring vision of Jesus offering her a wedding ring made of the foreskin from his circumcision. Saint María Maddelena de Pazzi licked the wounds of lepers.

If Sister María Rosa's modus operandi was unorthodox, it again echoed the behavior of her order's beloved Saint Francis. The writer G. K. Chesterton called Francis "eccentric, in that he turned always toward the center." Francis's eccentricities, according to legend, included wearing rags and speaking with beasts. Sister María Rosa's eccentricities included her gall in chasing down Honduras's richest man aboard a plane, her stubbornness in swimming into hurricane floodwaters toward the cry of a child no one else heard, her laser-beam focus on the dignity of mothers and the needs of poor children. Her behavior was an outward sign of her turning, like Saint Francis, toward her own center and not toward any social customs or societal norms. People just don't *do* the things she did nor behave in the indomitable way she did. Sister María Rosa's focus folded inward to what she perceived to be God's plan, to where she discerned God's blueprint. Considering that—plus the fact that she spent her formative years in the shelter of the convent, unexposed to secular conventions—she was remarkably effective at getting things done her way in the world today.

When we talk about goodness, we often assign that quality to a person or an act in retrospect, after we have seen the long-term positive results. Goodness in action or goodness of the moment can look like something else entirely: a paradox of sometimes risky behavior, albeit with a beneficial intention. An untraditional trajectory of virtue, however, can still have a marvelous, admirable outcome, and for this reason, lots of people still yearn to affiliate their own efforts with Sister María Rosa's extraordinary results. Who wouldn't want to join Team María Rosa? It's hard to resist the pull of her great goodness, her passionate love for the poor, her hard-won victories. She was a rock star of good works. Visitors and Hondurans alike fell over themselves loving her children and sitting close to her so that her holiness might rub off on them, that they might take some grace home in their suitcases and their hearts.

Several announcements of Sister María Rosa's death on social media featured this phrase: *Hay una fiesta en el cielo!* (There is a party in heaven!) No one at SAN doubts that Sister Maria Rosa was worthy of a ticket straight to heaven. She herself liked to talk about the price for Paradise.

"I don't know what kind of money you need in heaven: lempiras or dollars or what?" she mused. "But the Lord is so good to accept our work or love or sacrifice. We can go to Him with empty hands. We only need the good we do for others and with others. That's the price for heaven, I think."

EPILOGUE

--"The Holy Spirit follows me around. Poor thing. He really will be a palomita, *a little bird, with no feathers left, I'm pulling so hard on them!"--*

Wr hen I first encountered Sister María Rosa Leggol on a short-term mission trip with my Catholic parish, I was a 42-year-old journalist-*cum*-stay-at-home-mom. The mission experience was meant to be just a one-week, one-time eye-opener to poverty and social injustice in the Third World. I thought the work might jar me from the idyll of my sturdy brick house in a tree-lined neighborhood in the affluent United States, where I had the sheer luck to be born. It was a simple notion to enlarge my world, flex my muscles, and open a little wider my wallet and my heart. Instead, that trip rearranged my life unexpectedly, uncomfortably—and perfectly.

I want to avoid offering easy platitudes about God's blueprint when His big picture is certainly more complex and mysterious than I can fathom. After years of listening to Sister María Rosa's certainty in God's plan, however, I began to notice perhaps some divine direction in my own life. Was it God's plan that I suffered the loss of my journalism career as I stayed home to raise kids, only to be available to write this book? Did the experience of adopting our youngest daughter from Guatemala give me an affinity for Latin American people that helped me understand Honduran idiosyncrasies and Third World culture? Did the supernatural events in Sister María Rosa's life pique my excitement so strongly because I once had my own improbable experience of "divine interruption" while driving in a snowstorm? Did the conflicting emotions of that "drop-in" from God—the heart-racing shock crossed with bottomless peace, the doubt that I was worthy bisected by the conviction that I am loved —prepare me to believe that God intervened in Sister María Rosa's work?

Sister María Rosa would smile and shrug at these questions, of course, and declare that every bit of it is God's plan. "Who can tell me that even back when I was six years old, it was not in God's plan that I would be doing this today?" she said often. "Who can tell these young men and women who come here to volunteer that it was not in God's mind when they were tiny children that one day they would come here and be part of this family? If you are here, somehow He wants you to be here!"

Sister María Rosa's ironclad trust in God's plan gave me and countless others faith in our own place within her mission. We found ourselves all aboard for SAN's wild ride, like the T-shirt that reads "Honduran Rules of the Road: Blind curves are ideal for passing." Sister María Rosa drove

SAN's vision at breakneck speed, passing the plodding vehicles of planning and fundraising and budgeting. Her mission teams and partner NGOs rode shotgun, not knowing what was lying around the curves, but trusting that they were in the right place at the right time.

To me, Sister María Rosa was not only a fearless rescuer of Honduras's poorest children, but a charismatic conduit of God's plan. For those of us who arrived in Honduras only to find ourselves thrown off balance by our first real encounter with such extreme poverty, she played God's Foreman: She pointed us toward purposeful tasks we never would have thought to venture or offer. Certainly every North American who travels on a mission trip to a Third World country comes back changed. For some, however, Sister María Rosa's invitation resulted in extraordinary callings to action that have made us whirl our life plans around, tack in an unexpected direction, and take on months or years of work we never expected to do.

A Milwaukee shipping magnate built Sister María Rosa a rural hospital.

A college student brought a blind Honduran baby to the United States to get eye surgery and a chance at life.

A rich Beverly Hills law associate gave up a lavish life in California to come home to Honduras and shepherd SAN's volunteers.

An oral surgeon from Ontario repeatedly emptied out his family's bank account to fund an NGO to support SAN.

Two short-term SAN volunteers devoted lifelong careers to Central American migrants and at-risk children.

A chef answered the call to become a priest.

A Nicaraguan teacher left her beloved classroom to advocate for SAN child sponsorships.

A law school graduate raised by SAN founded a medical brigade organization to practice Sister María Rosa's teachings in rural Honduras.

Two business executives commissioned an artistic film to promote Sister María Rosa's work.

And I wrote a book about Sister María Rosa's life, her against-all-odds achievements, and the way she drew in all the right people to support her mission of love, hope and redemption.

The list could go on and on.

Our transformation feels a little like one of the Mini-Extreme Home Makeovers my mission groups perform on SAN's children's homes—it feels as if Sister María Rosa somehow maneuvered herself into the left atrium of our hearts and started rearranging heavy furniture. We experience a shifting, a banging around, an unsettling of plans and priorities. We have trouble articulating exactly why we keep dipping deep into our vacation time, bank accounts, and fortitude to return to Sister María Rosa's mission again and again. We do these things for the benefit of SAN and the Honduran children we love, but the work feels personal, even holy, called forth out of our individual abilities and talents, the innate presence of God inside us. In this work for her mission we find our own version of Sister María Rosa's "dignity of life" and possibly our own pathway to heaven. Sister María Rosa may or may not eventually be named a saint, but this is exactly what saints do: They point us toward heaven.

"She always encouraged you to serve in a way that let you use the unique gifts that you have," concluded Father Jeff Godecker, the Indianapolis priest who founded his parish's outreach mission to Honduras in 1999.

There is a verse by Thomas Merton, the contemplative monk and social activist, that for me illustrates how we are all bound to Sister María Rosa, Honduras, the children, and each other in our efforts:

I am a link in the chain of light and presence.

Maybe we, in all our disparate homelands and various efforts, are somehow linked together in Sister María Rosa's chain of good works in Honduras. If Sister María Rosa is represented here by *light*—the light of her vision for a hopeful future for all the vulnerable children of Honduras—could our portion be *presence,* simply showing up to work with her and her children and to carry out our God-gifted assignments? Showing up sounds easy, but it is an enormous challenge to continue to attend this mission again and again and stay present in the tension, despair, and violence of poverty, straddling the wide disparity between our lives in America or Canada and theirs in the Third World. The short-term mission trip became a lifelong vocation for some of us, with no compartmentalization of the mission experience tucked away from our day-to-day lives. Through our little chain-links of work, however, we have been privileged to witness and honor Honduran lives of hope and dignity and grace.

One note about my own link of work, writing about Sister María Rosa: My "assignment from God" seemed straightforward at first, but then I hit a roadblock. There is a saying that all stories are true, and some actually happened. As a listener to Sister María Rosa's stories, like everyone else I was rapt and enchanted. As a journalist trying to transcribe details, however, I wanted to tear out my hair over the shifting accuracy of "facts"—dates, numbers, and names that changed with the retelling of any anecdote. Even as I spent hours crunching numbers of SAN's children's homes and projects over the years in an attempt to account for 40,000 unique children raised by SAN over 50 years, Sister María Rosa began telling the Honduran media that the number was now 87,000. I began to realize that a rigorous fact-check of Sister María Rosa's story would be utterly impossible: Most sources for Sister María Rosa's early history are word-of-mouth, and much of it is from Sister María Rosa herself. More than once, the editor in my head concluded I could not write this book, because I couldn't hope to get the details exactly right.

As I continued to absorb beautiful stories of lives transformed, however, I eventually came to accept—and even celebrate—that colorful, fabulous Latin culture that exaggerates details and fudges facts even as it honors the gist of the story. Absolutes are maddeningly slippery in Honduras, but there is still truth in the gray areas. So if some of Sister María Rosa's recollections or my retelling of them are not 100 percent precise in particular, they are still true in general. I did my very best with accuracy, but even my own reporting on Sister María Rosa is colored by my own background and experiences and by the fact that I am culturally a *Norteamericana*.

I'll leave you with one last word about accuracy. Writing about Sister María Rosa's childhood, I felt awkward using her religious name rather than her birth name. She was not born "María Rosa." Like the rest of us, she was a child once, and she has a gorgeous Honduran birth name. She abandoned that name, however, when she became a Sister and took the names María, for the Mother of God, and Rosa, for

Saint Rose of Lima. She felt so strongly about this name business that after Vatican II, when many religious women reverted to their birth names, she changed her name legally to María Rosa so she could keep it.

"I don't miss that other name," she told me. "After I became María Rosa, I did not care to have the other one. If I renounce the world, I am renouncing everything of my former life, including my old name. I think because God changed me into a Sister and I was consecrated on the altar with the name María Rosa, I should keep it. When I go to heaven, I know the Lord will be calling me María Rosa, so I should answer to that!"

I decided to stick with María Rosa throughout this book, too. I figure if people ever want to pray to her in heaven for intercessions, they had better call her Sister María Rosa or she won't listen.

When I think of Sister María Rosa's life adventures and crusades, I like to imagine that she caught a frequent ride on the Holy Spirit. Her description of the Holy Spirit—"Poor thing. He really will be a little *palomita* with no feathers left; I'm pulling so hard on them!"—stopped me in my tracks the first time I heard her say it. I immediately got the *palomita*— little bird—reference. The dove is a well-known symbol of the Spirit. But pulling feathers off? Stripping the bird? Who among us challenges the Holy Spirit, cries out, "Wait a minute!" and actually grabs onto the dove with clutching fingers? I think most of us would just listen in awe to the whispering whoosh of conscience and murmur, *Thank you.*

Then there is Sister María Rosa, who was not content with just a quiet wind in her ear. Instead she latched on tight and rode her Holy Spirit over a deep, dark lake of poverty and need. Hers was a lengthy journey—her lifelong battle to bring hope and dignity to the poor—and after awhile, her ill legs wouldn't carry her anymore. So she hopped on, trusted the bird completely, and went wherever it would take her.

HOW YOU CAN HELP SISTER MARIA ROSA'S MISSION

Sociedad Amigos de los Niños (SAN) follows the vision of its founder and works tirelessly for the benefit of at-risk children and adolescents in Honduras, the second poorest country in the Western Hemisphere.

Here are ways you can get involved with Sister María Rosa's continuing mission:

To sponsor a child or make a tax-deductible contribution in the United States, visit Friends of Honduran Children Indiana at www.fhcindiana.org.

In Canada, contact Friends of Honduran Children Canada at www.honduranchildren.com.

To learn more or to contribute directly to SAN in Honduras, visit their website at www.sanhn.org.

Two additional U.S. NGOs, Honduran Children's Rescue Fund (www.honduranchildrensrescuefund.org) and Virtú Inc. (www.virtuinc.org), do great work with SAN, too.

A portion of this book's proceeds will be donated to SAN.

ACKNOWLEDGMENTS

Mil gracias to all the Hondurans who hosted this *gringa*, explained things both obvious and inscrutable to me, and offered insight into SAN and Honduras: Mae Valenzuela, Carolina Agüero Agurcia, Sonia Erazo, Pancho Paz, Cato Elvir, Quique Rodriguez, Alejandra Lorenzana, Santa Barahona, Evelyn Casco, and most of all, Sister María Rosa, who welcomed me, with or without mission groups in tow, to sit at her table for 13 years. Gracias, Armando Cordova, Rene Caceres, and the Ponce brothers for safety and friendship; Juani Esperanza Arriaga, Aleyda Tinoco, and Yesica Lemus for handmade tortillas, fried plantains, and fresh strawberry juice; Doña Rosa María Ortiz, Ana Ramirez, and dear Mercedes Rodriguez for their Nuevo Paraíso care; and the Vigilantes for guarding us and the precious children of SAN. Special thanks to Kevin Zazo for laughter, bear hugs, his heartfelt care of Sister in her final days, and his illuminating explanation of what it really means when a Honduran says he will definitely come to your party!

I am forever grateful to my husband and children, who accommodated my weeklong trips to Honduras once, then twice, then four times a year. Thank you, Annie and Patrick, for coming to Honduras with me on young adult mission trips and to Cece, whose young childhood birthday celebrations were delayed because of my annual winter dates in Honduras (until I schemed to change the week of our parish mission trips). Thank you, Scoop, for choosing Honduras for many of your surgery mission trips; I can't wait till we can travel to the same place in Honduras at the same time.

Thanks to my parents and sister who have always facilitated my wanderlust, starting with my study-abroad year in Austria, and for listening to all my rants and raves about my Honduras trips. My parents also unwittingly fed my fascination with nuns by sending me to Catholic schools for first grade through university. My sister, Angie Mattingly of Envision Ideas, spent untold hours of brilliant design work on my author website; she is masterful—and my closest friend.

Blessings and love to friend and mentor Father Jeff Godecker, who founded Immaculate Heart of Mary (IHM) Parish's Honduras mission to transport us out of the idyll of suburban Indianapolis and open our hearts to relationships with the Third-World poor. Thanks for counseling me on early iterations of the book and nudging me onward. Thanks go also to Father Bob Sims, current pastor of Immaculate Heart, who wholeheartedly supports our Honduras mission trips and even allowed me to send parish money down to SAN when we couldn't travel there in person during the pandemic.

Very special thanks to the wonderful Carolina Agüero Agurcia, who continues to devote much of her life to SAN's children and who hand-delivered this book to Cardinal Rodriguez, shepherded his Foreword back to me, and helped proofread my English translation.

I owe huge gratitude to my early, middle, and late readers. Janet Hock, your enthusiasm and advice about reaching a wider-than-just-Catholic audience has been invaluable. I believe you first coined "serial entrepreneur" in describing Sister María Rosa, and now it has spread far and wide! Thank you, Monica Lewis, Kelly Molloy, Suzanne Jannetta, and Page Zyromski for great ideas and suggestions, and to Dan Coyle for encouragement about publishing and tips about writing cinematically. I appreciate those who generously gave their time to read this book and offer advanced reviews: Diana Negroponte, Fathers Dan Groody and Jeff Godecker, and Doctor Chuck Dietzen.

Greg Cliburn, editor extraordinaire, taught me much of what I know about writing and editing when we worked together at *Outside Magazine*. Thank you for treating my book baby with your trademark wisdom and respect, and for helping decide on the pesky spelling for the plural of Honduras. Cover designer Peter Selgin did a brilliant job and was patient with all my early title changes; I'm so happy he worked on this book.

Deep appreciation goes to generous photographers David Mangurian and Johannes Frick for use of their gorgeous pictures in this book and its companion book of quotes, *Always Room For One More* (Cornelia Avenue Press, 2022). Thanks also to SAN, Miraflores Films, and the School Sisters of Saint Francis for permission to use their photos of Sister María Rosa. Thanks, Nicole Bernardi-Reis, for offering me access to the Sor María Rosa Archives. All pictures of Sister became so much more precious to me after she died and I felt joy every moment I spent with these works of art and history.

Thanks to all the profile subjects in this book who shared their beautiful personal dramas of the effect Sister María Rosa had on their lives. Their impressions and stories provide bold color and perspective to people who never met Sister and they highlight so many of her faces, moods, and roles: miracle worker, mentor, and even matchmaker!

Blessings and love to everyone who sponsors a SAN child or travels to Honduras to help Sister's kids, especially my IHM Honduras mission teams and my Friends of Honduran Children Indiana family. You lent me unique and varied lenses through which to see Sister María Rosa—especially the youth groups, always surprised by their first impressions of Sister ("She's so humble! She's so funny! She's so self-deprecating, not like a nun at all!") Thanks for the loving actions, sweaty labor, "volcanic" cement mixing, impactful daily reflections, yummy Price-Smart brownies, yummier Salva Vidas, bad jokes, wild Euchre games, gut-busting jags of laughter, and most especially the nightly music jams capped by the *Wagon Wheel* sing-along.

Finally, thanks, God, for setting the pick for me for so long. I was busy driving carpools and doing the managerial work of running a family, but you kept the story revving in my heart and head—with unyielding persistence reminiscent of our favorite Honduran nun.

P.S. I would be so grateful if readers would consider posting a review on this book's product page at the online bookstore where you purchased it. Reviews are essential for boosting exposure and spreading the word about Sister María Rosa's epic achievements in Honduras. I read every review! If you cannot leave a reader review online, send it to me via email at kmo@kathymartinoneil.com.

PHOTO CREDITS

Robert Arsenault: Page 105 (top)

David Bower: Page 12 (bottom)

Colleen D'Angelo: Page 204

Cato Elvir Fontecha: Page 201

Johannes Frick: Pages 12 (top), 218 (bottom), 240 (top)

Alby Glassmeyer: Page 223

Father Jeff Godecker: Page 170 (top)

Larry Hildebrand: Page 131

LIFE en Espanol Magazine (Feb 26, 1968): Page 67 (top)

David Mangurian: Cover, page 10

Father Hector Mateus-Ariza: Page 219

Guillermo José Matus Castellón: Page 107

Doctor Jim McCallum: Page 70

Courtesy of Miraflores Films: Pages 217 (bottom), 250 (both), 251 (both)

Chameli Naraine: Page 197

Kathy Martin O'Neil: Pages xxvi (both), 22 (top), 90 (top), 170 (bottom), 217 (top), 241 (bottom), 253, 254, 255 (both), 263, 265, back cover

Doctor Norman Powell: Page 52

Gerardo Enrique Rodriguez: Pages 151, 195 (middle), 241 (top)

School Sisters of Saint Francis: Pages 21, 22 (bottom), 33, 34 (both), 50 (bottom), 69 (bottom)

Brian Smith: Page 176

Sociedad Amigos de los Niños: Pages xvii, 11 (both), 35 (both), 36, 50 (top), 51 (both), 67 (bottom), 68 (both), 69 (top), 89 (both), 90 (bottom), 91, 104 (both), 105 (bottom), 106 (both), 124 (both), 125 (both), 126 (both), 127, 149 (both),

150 (both), 169 (bottom), 195 (top and bottom), 196 (both), 218 (top), 240 (bottom), 242

Susan Weber: Page 169 (top), 171

ABOUT THE AUTHOR

Kathy Martin O'Neil is a writer, mission trip leader, and the author of two books about Sister María Rosa: *Madre: The Nun Who Was Mother to the Orphans of Honduras* (Cornelia Avenue Press, 2022) and the upcoming *Always Room For One More: Wit and Wisdom from the Mother Teresa of Honduras* (Cornelia Avenue Press, 2022). She is the former managing editor of *Outside Magazine* and Rand McNally's editorial book division, with degrees from the University of Notre Dame and Northwestern's Medill School of Journalism. Her 30 trips to Honduras and counting have sparked keen interest in Latin

American culture, inventive fruit juices, salty Spanish words, reggaeton music, devotion to the Virgin Mary, and the dangerous situation for migrant children at the U.S. border. In her spare time between driving kids around she writes a little music, sings and plays banjo and bodhrán in a band called the Crooked Finger Rhythm Revue, leads music at church, and sings Alto 2 with the Indianapolis Symphonic Choir. She resides with her family in Indianapolis, Indiana, the Crossroads of America, after stints in Chicago, Santa Fe, Toronto, and Innsbruck, Austria. Visit her website for additional adoration of Honduras and thoughts about short-term mission travel at www.kathymartinoneil.com.

Made in United States
North Haven, CT
11 July 2022

21198042R00163